Dear Reader:

The book you are about to read is the latest bestseller from the St. Martin's True Crime Library, the imprint the *New York Times* calls "the leader in true crime!" Each month, we offer you a fascinating account of the latest, most sensational crime that has captured the national attention. St. Martin's is the publisher of perennial bestselling true crime author Jack Olsen whose SALT OF THE EARTH is the true story of one woman's triumph over life-shattering violence; Joseph Wambaugh called it "powerful and absorbing." Fannie Weinstein and Melinda Wilson tell the story of a beautiful honors student who was lured into the dark world of sex for hire in THE COED CALL GIRL MURDER. St. Martin's is also proud to publish critically acclaimed author Carlton Stowers, whose 1999 Edgar Award-winning TO THE LAST BREATH recounts a two-year-old girl's mysterious death, and the dogged investigation that led loved ones to the most unlikely murderer: her own father. In the book you now hold, CRADLE OF DEATH, John Glatt explores a series of tragic infant deaths, and the trail that led to their mother.

St. Martin's True Crime Library gives you the stories *behind* the headlines. Our authors take you right to the scene of the crime and into the minds of the most notorious murderers to show you what really makes them tick. St. Martin's True Crime Library paperbacks are better than the most terrifying thriller, because it's all true! The next time you want a crackling good read, make sure it's got the St. Martin's True Crime Library logo on the spine—you'll be up all night!

Charles E. Spicer, Jr.
Senior Editor, St. Martin's True Crime Library

"I SUFFOCATED HER."

Back alone at N. American Street with Constance, Marie decided to celebrate her baby's one-month anniversary by training her to sit up in a chair. Placing the tiny baby on a chair in the parlor, she arranged one pillow behind her and set another chair in front to support her so she wouldn't topple over. Suddenly Constance began to cry and Marie lost control.

"I don't know why," she would later confess, "but then I took a pillow and laid her down on the chair and I suffocated her."

Then in a dream-like state Marie carefully carried Constance to her crib and closed her eyes as if she was asleep. Then she left the room and went upstairs to the bathroom to compose herself. There she remained until she heard her husband come through the front door.

ST. MARTIN'S TRUE CRIME LIBRARY TITLES BY JOHN GLATT

For I Have Sinned

Evil Twins

Cradle of Death

CRADLE OF DEATH

JOHN GLATT

St. Martin's Paperbacks

CRADLE OF DEATH

Copyright © 2000 by John Glatt.

Cover photograph courtesy David Fields / Sygma.

All rights reserved. No part of this book may be used or reproduced in any manner whatsoever without written permission except in the case of brief quotations embodied in critical articles or reviews. For information address St. Martin's Press, 175 Fifth Avenue, New York, N.Y. 10010.

ISBN: 0-312-97302-0

Printed in the United States of America

St. Martin's Paperbacks edition / March 2000

10 9 8 7 6 5 4 3 2 1

FOR THE NOE BABIES

ACKNOWLEDGMENTS

The Marie Noe case is perhaps one of the most bizarre and intriguing murder mysteries in the annals of American criminology. Spanning a full half century, it began in 1949 when Harry Truman was in the White House and would finally see closure only at the dawn of the twenty-first century.

I first read about Marie Noe in *The New York Times* after her arrest and, like many, found it hard to fathom how a mother could possibly murder eight of her own children in cold blood and evade justice for so long.

As I dug deeper and deeper into the strange story of Marie Noe, with its tangled webs of deceit through the 1950s and 1960s, I saw so many occasions when she might have been unmasked for the untold evil she wrought. When it finally looked as if she might be caught by a crack team of investigators from the medical examiner's office, she managed to convince Philadelphia homicide detectives of her innocence. Then along came Sudden Infant Death Syndrome, which provided a near-perfect alibi for the next thirty years.

I spent a year researching this highly complex case, reading scores of the original case files and tracking down many of the key investigators, pathologists and Noe family members still alive.

I am particularly indebted to Jamie Talan and her husband Richard Firstman who proved invaluable to the project by generously providing me background and insight. It was their award-winning book on the Waneta Hoyt case, *Death of Innocents* that ultimately led to the arrest and conviction of Marie Noe.

I would also like to thank Dr. Stuart Asch and Dr. Halbert Fillinger for all their patience and help during the months of research. Marie's sister, Anne Danielski, who remains convinced of her innocence, also spoke to me at length on several occasions about Marie's childhood and family life.

Vince Ziemba of the Philadelphia Criminal Justice Center proved invaluable by showing me Kensington first-hand and giving me a full historical background of the unique neighborhood that plays an integral role in the Noe story.

Much thanks also goes to D.A. Lynne Abraham and her former press secretary Bill Davol, Mary Cadwalader, Dr. Robert Catherman, Dr. Dimitri Contostavlos, Meki Cox, Dr. Salvatore Cucinotta, Regina Farrell, Lillian Harper, Nicholas Maxymuik, Joe McGillen, Sergeant Larry Nodiff, Dr. Linda Norton, Ron Avery, Detective Joseph Schimpf, Sister Michael Marie, Dr. Molly Valdes-Dapena, Dr. Laurie Varlotta, Violetta Zimba and the many others I spoke with who wanted to remain anonymous.

I would also like to thank my editor Charles Spicer, who first drew my attention to the original *New York Times* story about Marie Noe and encouraged me to pursue it. My gratitude also goes to my agent Peter Miller, and all at the PMA Film and Literary Agency, for their constant support.

Other debts are owed to Wensley Clarkson, Susan Chenery, Annette Witheridge, Fred and Linda Wehner, Roger Hitts, Chris Bowen and Daphna Inbar.

CONTENTS

"She was almost a face in shadows. We never knew very much about her. She was nothing special, just a mother and a housewife from a row house neighborhood. There was nothing that made Marie Noe really stand out except that all her babies died."

—Dr. Halbert E. Fillinger, Jr., M.D., City of Philadelphia Assistant Medical Examiner 1960–1988.

CRADLE OF
DEATH

PROLOGUE

On the morning of Wednesday, August 5, 1998, Philadelphia District Attorney Lynne M. Abraham marched into a packed press conference to clarify a mystery that had confounded the city for almost half a century. Her communications director Bill Davol had previously put the word out to the media that they would be dealing with a tragic story of national proportions.

At nine o'clock a swarm of local affiliate and network TV crews and print reporters converged on the vast D.A.'s office building, across the road from the historic Liberty Bell. There, under the savage glare of television lights, Abraham looked deadly serious as she mounted the podium to begin. With her closely cropped silver hair, worn military-style, she resembled a field commander about to brief the troops.

For the next half-hour the tall, heavy-set woman whom *The New York Times* once dubbed "America's deadliest D.A.," would constantly refer to a giant poster board behind her to simplify the most convoluted murder investigation of her distinguished seven-year career. There, clearly set out in black and white, were the autopsy results of eight babies from a single Philadelphia family, who had died mysteriously over a nineteen-year period between 1949 and 1968.

It was a baffling series of deaths which had defied explanation. Although over the years some had suspected foul play, it had taken half a century for the Philadelphia police to make their move and reopen the investigation. And now the publicity-savvy Abraham, soon expected to announce a run for mayor, was determined to maximize its impact.

Just three hours earlier homicide detectives had arrested Marie Noe, the now–sixty-nine-year-old mother of the babies, in her tenement row house in the tough Philadelphia suburb of Kensington. Four months earlier she had finally confessed and been booked on eight counts of first-degree murder. Now the frail, white-haired senior citizen stood to become notorious as the most prolific serial baby-killer in American history.

Fully aware that the arrest would be very high-profile indeed, D.A. Abraham's carefully stage-managed announcement fully reflected its gravity.

"When Theodore Dreiser wrote a novel called *An American Tragedy*, he never knew or conceived of a case like this," she declared. "For the dead children, this case involves a great American tragedy." A few days later one of her assistant D.A.'s, Jay Feinschi, would go even further, placing Marie Noe squarely in the company of the infamous serial killer Ted Bundy.

The Noe babies had started dying in 1949 when the Baby Boom was in full swing and Harry Truman was President of the United States. In the staunchly blue-collar district of Kensington, a twenty-year-old newly-wed named Marie Noe gave birth to her first child, Richard Allan, who weighed a healthy seven pounds, eleven ounces. Exactly one month later Marie's factory-worker husband Arthur came home from work to find the baby dead in his crib.

Richard's' death was the beginning of a tragedy of epic proportions that would span the next two decades, as Marie Noe gave birth to a total of ten babies. Incredibly, eight died in unexplained circumstances at home, none surviving for more than fifteen months and many dying within days or weeks of birth.

After the untimely death of the seventh Noe baby, Mary Lee, Marie Noe was featured under a pseudonym in a 1963 *Life* magazine story, anointing her America's most famous bereaved mother. The highly sympathetic story cast Marie and Arthur Noe in the roles of courageous victims of an unspeakable medical mystery, although *Life* writer Mary Cadwalader would later admit that Marie's total lack of emotion while discussing her dead babies had made her secretly question whether the deaths had been accidental.

Cadwalader wasn't the only one to ask that terrible question. Doctors, forensic pathologists and even the Philadelphia medical examiner of the day all harbored strong doubts about Marie Noe. But with the newly defined condition Sudden Infant Death Syndrome (SIDS) captivating the American public in the 1960s, no one dared go out on a limb and risk career ruin by accusing a mother of committing the unspeakable crime of murdering her own babies.

Five years later when the last Noe baby, Arthur Joseph, perished at just five months of age, Marie had a hysterectomy and closed the book on her babies for more than thirty years.

But in the 1990s the notion that multiple SIDS death could run in families was scientifically debunked. Now the moral pendulum had swung the other way, with several mothers like Waneta Hoyt and Mary Beth Tinning being successfully prosecuted for serial infanticide. Now, at long last, the spotlight was shining on the biggest case of all.

In March 1998, Marie Noe had finally broken her

silence to confess the terrible secrets she had locked away for so many years. Even hardened detectives were shocked by Marie's apparent lack of emotion and contrition, as she chillingly admitted smothering four of her babies to death. Then, almost apologetically, she explained that it had been so long ago, she couldn't remember if she had harmed the others, although, she admitted, it was quite possible.

"When you have two, three, four, five, six, seven, eight deaths in one family, this is not SIDS," D.A. Abraham told a network television reporter after her conference. "This is not unexplained. This is not undetermined. This is homicide!" Her prosecutors, she said, would seek a life sentence as the current death-penalty law had not been passed at the time of the babies' deaths.

But the seeds of one of America's most baffling and terrifying serial murders go back to the last century, when Marie Noe's grandparents first arrived in Philadelphia as young immigrants pursuing the American dream.

PART ONE

THE KILLINGS

ONE

SEEDS OF EVIL

At the end of the last century Philadelphia was a thriving metropolis, bursting at the seams with European immigrants, seeking a fresh start in a new land of unlimited opportunity. Once the capital of the United States and the presidential home of George Washington, the picturesque city, strategically perched on the banks of the Schuylkill River, had long since relinquished power to Washington, D.C.

New opportunities had sprung up in the wake of the Industrial Revolution and America's fourth largest city now pushed outwards to accommodate wave after wave of new immigrants. Many of them headed straight for the suburb of Kensington where they'd heard jobs were plentiful in the flourishing new textile mills.

Founded in 1730 by an English merchant seaman named Anthony Palmer, Kensington had started life as a riverfront fishing village and was named after one of London's most fashionable areas. According to local legend, Charles Dickens passed through in 1842 and dubbed it Fishtown, a nickname that is still in use today.

Right from the beginning the district had carved out its own identity, setting it apart from its big brother, Philadelphia. Kensington would always be more a state of mind than a geographical location. And with its narrow, twisting streets of plain, tightly packed row houses, it quickly evolved into a close-knit neighborhood with an intense distrust of outsiders.

In the early 1800s life in Kensington was all about survival. The new Irish Catholic immigrants either eked out a living from the Schuylkill, building boats or fishing for herring, or they stayed at home and weaved linen on hand looms. And there was much resentment between the weavers and their rich English Protestant employers, who lived in lavish houses in the smarter parts of Philadelphia.

Tavern brawls were common between the fiercely patriotic Irish immigrants and their English and German neighbors who looked down on them. Violence always lay just below the surface and once a slight about "bloody Irish transports" had led to a two-day riot that had to be quelled by the army.

But the tide turned in 1830 when a carpet factory set up in the district, bringing with it a new prosperity. It was soon followed by the construction of America's first textile mill, with many more following in its wake. The new mills created thousands of new jobs in Kensington, quickly establishing it as the textile capital of America.

By the 1880s Kensington had become the industrial heart of Philadelphia with more than one hundred textile mills, employing thousands of new immigrants, including young children. John B. Stetson opened a huge factory on Lehigh Avenue to make his fashionable felt cowboy hats and just a few blocks away was the world's largest lace factory.

It was into this alluring industrial gold rush, with its promise of steady employment, that a teenage servant girl named Mary McBride arrived in the late 1800s, fleeing the poverty and starvation of her native Ireland. Far away from home and her family, the pretty blonde immigrant soon found lodgings in West Kensington and employment in a nearby textile mill.

Before long Mary had caught the attention of a strapping young man named John Lyddy, who had recently arrived from France where he had trained as a brewmaster. The two young immigrants began dating at a local taproom and had soon fallen in love.

In the fall of 1890 they were married in a Catholic ceremony in Philadelphia. The following June, Mary delivered a healthy baby boy whom she named James. The family settled down on Westmoreland Street where John supported his family as a factory warehouseman. Over the next few years Mary lost several babies in childbirth but did manage to produce two healthy ones, Harry and Alice.

The Lyddys were typical of their immigrant neighborhood, taking great pride in their new-found respectability. Indeed, it seemed that anything was possible in this new land of opportunity, if you just rolled up your sleeves and worked hard.

By the turn of the century, Kensington had become a staunchly working-class district where housewives took great pride in scrubbing down their front steps each morning. But although most Kensingtonians had never had it so good, there were dark clouds on the horizon for the Lyddys and their eldest son James, who did not share his parents' devotion to hard work.

James Lyddy always seemed to attract trouble from his earliest days. As a youngster he seldom attended school and was always in trouble with the law. During his early teens his father died suddenly of a heart attack, leaving the family penniless. And when his mother was forced to return to work in her early forties, James ran wild with no supervision.

Mary Lyddy was a hard-working, devoted mother, who looked forward to the day when her eldest son would get a job and ease her financial burden. But James had a mean, lazy streak and after leaving school he always found an excuse for living off his mother and not working. He preferred to sleep late, spending most afternoons in one of the new movie palaces on nearby Kensington Avenue, with their live stage shows, or watching a Phillies baseball game.

Although James was a mercurial young man with an uncontrollable, violent temper, he knew how to turn on the charm and could talk his way out of anything. His tall, brooding good looks made him popular with the local girls and he never lacked female companionship.

The textile mills were flourishing making the Kensington of the early 1900s a place of easy money which provided many distractions for a young man like James. There were taprooms on almost every corner and hard drinking was commonplace. But the dirty streets and packed houses were dwarfed by smelly factories which bred disease. Tuberculosis was rife, along with venereal diseases and high numbers of ragged illegitimate children. The young James ran wild with people who drowned their despair in alcohol. Habits formed then that would later impact on his daughter Marie.

Just before the outbreak of the First World War, twenty-three-year-old James had a passionate affair with a tall, young Irish-born girl named Ella Ackler, who was two months younger. Within a few weeks she had become pregnant and on May 25, 1914, Ella's angry parents insisted the couple marry in a traditional Roman Catholic church service.

The newlyweds settled down at 3520 N. 5th Street in Kensington but the honeymoon was short-lived. The indolent James resented being forced into marriage, refusing to accept any marital responsibilities or support his pregnant wife. Each morning he made great show of leaving for work but rarely arrived. Instead he headed to a taproom and got drunk with his cronies.

When the headstrong Ella caught him out and challenged him, he flew into a fury and walked out after a mere six weeks of marriage to move back in with his mother. But he had underestimated Ella's fiery Irish resolve and her determination to hold him to their marriage vows at any cost.

Calling his bluff, Ella went to the Domestic Relations Court, accusing her new husband of being a deadbeat and failing to support her. She impressed the judge by telling him that she had given James an ultimatum: either he provide a home for her within a week or the marriage was over.

Outmaneuvered, James backed down and agreed to face up to his responsibilities. He went home to Ella with his tail between his legs, promising to be a good husband from now on.

This would be the first of many times that Ella would resort to the courts in a long, torturous and often violent marriage that would leave a dreadful stamp on all their children.

As the First World War raged over in Europe, the textile mills in Kensington kept rolling. Business was booming and the district now led the United States in textile output, making everything from rugs and carpets to *haute couture* fashions. Things looked even brighter in 1922 with the opening of the new $15 million Frankford Elevated Line, connecting Kensington to downtown Philadelphia and promising even further business expansion in the area.

But although jobs were plentiful for anyone willing to do an honest day's work, James Lyddy lived in his own frivolous world, which did not include gainful employment or responsibility.

Ella's first pregnancy had ended tragically when she miscarried twins, but she delivered a healthy baby girl, Helen, in March 1917 and a second daughter, Anne, the following year. Being a father pushed James into brief employment with the Philadelphia Rapid Transit System but he soon went on extended sick leave, claiming the train fumes made him ill. And whenever Ella pleaded with him to look after the family, he would physically lash out at her, throwing screaming tantrums and walking out.

There were endless quarrels over James' drinking and laziness. He in turn would accuse Ella of having affairs with other men from the district. Time after time James would leave Ella and move back in with his mother, but somehow she always managed to persuade him to come home again. Inevitably, the reunions would always be short-lived.

This erratic pattern of behavior carried on unabated for the next decade as the dysfunctional relationship limped on. And although the marriage became increasingly violent, with Ella often wearing a scarf to hide her bruises from neighbors, there were passionate moments between fights, producing a stream of babies over the next few years.

A third daughter, Frances, was born in October 1921, followed by a son, Jimmy, in February 1923.

"After Jimmy was born my mother wasn't supposed to have any more children, according to the doctors," said their second-eldest daughter Anne. "Then Marie came along."

Marie Lyddy should never have been born. Ella had her tubes tied after Jimmy and did not expect or welcome any more children. Unwanted from the start, Marie was, nevertheless, born at home on August 23, 1928, during one of James Lyddy's many absences. It was a long and painful birth with a midwife in attendance.

A week before Marie's arrival her thirty-seven-year-old father had stormed out yet again after a violent argument, taking refuge with his mother just around the corner on N. Dillman Street. It would be weeks before he saw his new chubby, blonde-haired baby daughter.

"Marie was a happy little thing," remembers Anne, who was ten years older and helped raise her as a second mother. "She was a beautiful baby."

With five children to bring up alone, Ella had reached the end of her tether. Falling behind in the rent and struggling to feed the family, she was forced to move out of the apartment on North Dillman Street to nearby Orthodox Street in an infested slum in the West Kensington district then known as Cooperstown.

After Marie's birth James completely turned his back on Ella and the children, refusing to give them any money. So when Marie was just eight months old, Ella returned to court, seeking legal action to force James

Lyddy to support his family. This time the judge ordered James, now thirty-eight, to have a physical examination to see why he couldn't work.

On May 11, 1929, Lyddy was seen by a court-ordered physician. He claimed he was a sick man with a series of medical ailments, including a chronic cough and sporadic pains across his back and chest. He also said he was still feeling the effects of being "gassed" some years earlier, during a brief job with the Philadelphia Rapid Transit System.

Five weeks later Lyddy was summoned to court and ordered once again to support his family. Now, with the threat of imprisonment looming, he grudgingly agreed. But when James moved back with his wife and children the situation deteriorated even further. Most nights he would come home late, liquored-up and riled, to accuse Ella of having affairs. He would scream and curse at her in a savage fury, often beating her up in front of the children while they looked on in horror.

It was a terrible time for baby Marie and her brother and sisters, who were all traumatized by the violence. Their only chances for escape were summer vacations to their grandmother's country house in rural Pennsylvania. Here Marie would amuse herself with her dolls and go push-biking around the country with her elder sisters.

"These were the happiest times of our lives," said Anne. "All the little kids were growing up and Marie loved being out in the country in the fresh air."

Back in Kensington the Lyddys' family life had become so unbearable that James and Ella agreed to separate and split up the children. After one particularly violent row in the spring of 1930, Ella moved Helen and

Marie in with her parents on Bennington Street, while James took Anne, Frances, and Jimmy to a new apartment a few blocks away on W. Oriana Street.

Soon afterwards, when Ella was six months pregnant, the family briefly reunited. But within a week tempers were flaring and James took Anne with him back to his mother.

On July 1, 1930, Ella had her husband back in court for non-support. She claimed that even though he had found a well-paid job at the Nu Process Damp Wash Company, the family wasn't getting a cent. During an emotional hearing she told Judge Brown that she was in dire straits and begged him to place her children in foster homes.

Two weeks later the court ordered all the Lyddy children, with the exception of the eldest, Helen, to undergo medical and psychological examinations by Dr. William Drayton, Jr., of the Neuropsychiatric Division of the Municipal Court.

Marie, now two, was declared healthy but Dr. Drayton advised that her tonsils be removed. All the other children were found to be normal with the exception of Frances, who was diagnosed as "subnormal" and educationally "limited."

A week later, on July 23, the court committed Anne, Frances and James into the care of the Catholic Children's Bureau. But the court decided that two-year-old Marie was too young to be put into care and allowed her to stay with her mother.

Just six weeks after losing the children, Ella gave birth to her sixth and final baby, Jack, at Philadelphia General Hospital. Once again James briefly returned home to see his new son. But on October 18th, 1930, he decided to leave his family and Kensington once and for all and took a train to New York to start a new life.

Furious at her husband's behavior Ella got a warrant for his arrest, and before long police caught up with him in New York. They brought him back to Philadelphia in shackles and threw him in jail.

On November 7th Judge Bluett placed James Lyddy on probation with the proviso that he stay at home and take care of his children, who had recently been released from the Catholic Children's Bureau. But within two weeks Ella was in court again, claiming that James had left and was refusing to live with her.

She told the judge that after renting out two rooms for $12 for her and the children, he had moved back with his mother. When she had complained, James had told her that even if he was sent to prison, he would be out in five days and she would get nothing.

Now, turning her back on her husband, Ella took financial matters into her own hands. She found a job in a mill, working nights from 2:00 a.m. to 10:00 a.m. for $15 a week (which would be worth $140 today), and hired a nanny named Mrs. Bears for $6 a week to look after little Marie while she was at work.

But by January 1931, Ella found the demands of working the night shift and coping with her children during the day too demanding and gave up the job. She went on relief and received $5 a week from the Philadelphia Department of Assistance. Once again James was hauled into court to explain why he still wasn't supporting his family. And yet again he persuaded the judge that he would do so and pay off his arrears. The judge agreed to his offer and discharged him. But true to form he never paid Ella a cent.

Over the next six months James' silver tongue and empty promises kept him out of prison. But on June 10th his luck ran out and he was given a ninety-day prison sentence for non-support.

With Ella having no means of supporting her six children, the welfare services now intervened to investigate the family and see what was going wrong. A week after their father entered the House of Correction, Marie and her nine-month-old brother Jack were examined by Dr. Alice E. John, a psychiatrist appointed by the Court Juvenile Division of Philadelphia. In her official report Dr. John described Marie as "a normal child but not well-trained" and Jack as "looking dull but not feeble-minded."

Six weeks later, the very same day that their elder sister Anne was discharged back to her mother, Marie and Jack were committed to an orphanage run by the Catholic Children's Bureau. Marie passed her third birthday there—alone.

Two months later on October 14, 1931, the two youngest Lyddy children were discharged from the care of the juvenile court, as their father was released from jail. Once again James swore to mend his ways and Ella agreed to write off the $571 arrears he owed her.

For the first time in years the Lyddys were a complete family and James found them a new apartment at 3541 Germantown Avenue, Kensington, and began looking for a job.

It would be a brief lull before a series of catastrophes that would rock the family for generations.

TWO

A FAMILY BATTLEFIELD

The Wall Street crash of 1929 and the depression that followed brought Kensington to its knees, along with the rest of industrial America. Banks collapsed, textile factories closed their doors and thousands of workers were suddenly unemployed. Lines of jobless men walking their families to the new soup kitchens became a common sight and Kensingtonians braced themselves for the hard times ahead.

In January 1933 a Philadelphia *Evening Bulletin* story perfectly captured the air of desperation and despair that now permeated every corner of the Lyddys' neighborhood.

"Here are darkened mills, here are shivering people crying for clothes and shoes those mills could give. But no money."

If life had been hard for the Lyddys before the Depression it was now considerably worse. James' moods grew even darker and Ella stopped pressuring him into work, as jobs were impossible to find.

James and Ella now argued for weeks at a time and all the violence and screaming took a heavy toll on the children, particularly the youngest, Marie and Jack. Their lives had been a revolving door of new apartments and orphanages which had scarred them irreparably during their formative years.

In 1932, in the midst of the Depression, four-year-old Marie caught scarlet fever and lapsed into a coma. She was taken to a hospital by Ella and her sister Anne with a fever of 105 degrees and almost died.

"I remember the doctors talking to my mother about Marie but I couldn't understand what they were saying as I was too young," said Anne, who was ten at the time. "My mother signed the papers and they brought [Marie] around to consciousness with a blood transfusion."

But when Marie finally left the hospital two months later, her family noticed a marked change in her personality. She was now as quiet as the grave and totally withdrawn, as if in her own world. Her once-rosy cheeks were drained of color and she appeared mentally slow.

"The doctors said that the scarlet fever had affected her brain," said Anne. "She was never the same again."

Many years later Marie would tell *Philadephia* magazine writer Stephen Fried that the doctors had given her a cocktail of experimental drugs, causing irreparable brain damage.

"I guess it took a toll on my . . . um, noodle," she quipped. "And as I got older I got worse."

This would be the first in a series of tragedies that befell the Lyddy children over the next decade and would warp Marie's life—with dire consequences for her future children.

Less than a year later Frances Lyddy was brutally raped by a forty-year-old neighbor, who had lured her to an empty house. Traumatized, the twelve-year-old ran home in tears and her mother went straight to the police. The rapist was soon caught and later sentenced to up to three years in jail.

Their daughter's rape had a sobering effect on James

and Ella Lyddy and they decided to move a few blocks away to 3140 N. Carlisle Street to make a fresh start. Their new home was in a better part of Kensington and a step up from their old apartments. But yet again the Lyddy children found themselves having to make new friends in the Catholic School where their parents enrolled them.

At school Marie found herself becoming withdrawn and surly. Since coming out of the coma she felt different from everyone else. It seemed as though there was nothing behind her blue eyes. Her fellow pupils often teased her for the strange blank look she permanently wore. She also seemed an academic cripple, remaining at the bottom of the class, finding it totally impossible to do even the simplest sums or learn to read and write. "I was very, I guess you would call it hard to teach," she would later remember.

But the painfully shy, blonde-haired little girl also had an obsessive need to be the center of attention. And she soon discovered that although she couldn't compete with her classmates intellectually, she could draw sympathy and attention from her teachers by feigning sickness. And over the next few years she learned to turn imagined ailments into a disarming weapon to manipulate those around her into giving her her own way.

At home Marie was often physically punished by her parents. Her younger brother Jack was always getting into trouble and somehow Marie always took the blame. She hated and resented her parents, believing that she was the scapegoat for Jack's bad behavior.

Ella and James punished their children in a particularly brutal fashion. Marie would later accuse her parents of whipping her with a cat-o'-nine-tails, striking her with closed fists or striking her across the buttocks with a belt. The violence and cruelty that James and Ella had unleashed on each other for years was now being turned full-force on Marie and Jack.

"Our father really made us toe the mark," said Marie's elder sister Frances many years later. "[He was] too strict, I think."

Over the next few years James Lyddy worked sporadically as a truck driver, a mechanic and a janitor while Ella stayed at home being a mother and housewife. On the outside at least the Lyddys' dysfunctional marriage seemed relatively peaceful for the very first time, as they managed to stay out of the courts for a while. But behind closed doors things were getting even worse as James' drinking increased, exacerbating his terrible temper.

Tragedy struck the family again in 1936 when five-year-old Jack was run over by a car and taken to Episcopal Hospital with severe bruising to his head. While there he contracted scarlet fever and lapsed into a coma, as Marie had done a couple of years earlier. Jack remained unconscious for a week and was given blood transfusions to survive.

When Jack returned home he was wilder than ever and even his father's frequent whippings failed to rein him in. Over the next few years Jack ran away from home again and again and had several run-ins with the police before he was twelve.

On January 25, 1937, the Lyddys were hauled back into court when a concerned neighbor called the police to intervene in one of their arguments. Court documents revealed that although James and Ella had stayed together for several years they were "still quarreling endlessly," with James again accusing his wife of "running around with other men."

A week later Ella walked out on him and moved into a small apartment at 238 E. Elkhart Street, Kensington, with the children. Once again as tempers cooled the Lyddys reunited, but on March 3, 1938, Ella was back in court telling a judge that she wanted a divorce because of James' drunken beatings and obscene language in front of the children.

The Second World War unexpectedly revived Kensington's fortunes as factories worked overtime and its shipyard expanded to produce new battleships for the war effort. As U.S. soldiers were drafted to Europe, the textile factories fitted them out in uniforms. Money started pouring back into the area, with the local taprooms and restaurants getting so much business they could hardly cope.

Many of Kensington's young men went off to Europe to fight, including seventeen-year-old James Lyddy, Jr., who was drafted into the army. But soon after America entered the war, the Lyddy family was plunged into a potential scandal when on June 28, 1940, Marie's eldest sister Helen gave birth to an illegitimate daughter. The baby, who was named Geraldine, would be a dark family secret that could never be spoken about. James and Ella decided to raise Geraldine as their own child, telling friends and neighbors that Ella had given birth unexpectedly.

Over the next couple of years the three eldest Lyddy daughters, Helen, Anne and Frances, all married and moved away from home, leaving Marie to take care of baby Geraldine. It would be her first experience of looking after an infant and undoubtedly molded her views of motherhood.

At the age of fourteen—still in the fifth grade and unable to read or write—Marie dropped out of school and was ordered to find a job by her father. She was now expected to do a day's work and then come home to care for her two-year-old niece. It soon proved too much for the quiet, reclusive teenager, who could never let her true feelings show.

Whether or not Marie was sexually abused as a child remains a mystery. Her brother Jack would later tell detectives that Marie had been raped in her early teens by a coast guard, while the family were vacationing in Cape May, New Jersey. Many years later a psychiatrist would ask Marie if she had ever been a victim of sexual abuse. "No, no, no, not really unless I volunteered it," she replied cryptically.

Most nights Marie and her brother Jack would be left at home alone to look after Geraldine, while their parents went out drinking in a nearby taproom.

Later Jack was picked up by police in March 1943, for loitering suspiciously around a coast guard station at a Kensington pier, and his parents told the authorities they didn't want to have anything further to do with him. He was charged with "truancy and incorrigibility" and underwent a psychiatric evaluation by Dr. William Drayton.

Although Dr. Drayton's report described Jack as "normal" but with "dull intelligence," he was remanded by a court to Allentown State Hospital in Pennsylvania, where he was diagnosed as suffering from "posttraumatic personality disorder." He would spend the next three years at the hospital undergoing psychiatric treatment.

Now as the only Lyddy child left at home, Marie was miserable and finding it increasingly difficult to cope, without her older sisters as a buffer between her and her parents. Just before her first period at the age of fourteen she went temporarily blind with an acute migraine and thought she was going to die. Although her sight soon returned, she dreaded being premenstrual with the recurring headaches and brief periods of blindness she would endure for the rest of her child-bearing years. But she never told anyone, and would not seek medical help for her blindness for another six years.

That winter Marie's sister Helen, who had moved to Florida after her marriage a year earlier, lost a baby daughter from a severe case of measles. When Marie heard the news she decided to run away from home and go to the funeral.

A middle-aged neighbor happened to be driving to Florida, so Marie asked him for a ride. Before leaving they worked out a bizarre method of payment, where the pretty young teenager agreed to provide sexual favors in exchange for the ride. So during the three-day drive to Plant City, Florida, Marie lost her virginity at the age of fourteen on the back seat of his car by the side of a road.

By the time they arrived in Plant City the funeral had already taken place. But Helen and her new husband felt so sorry for the bedraggled Marie when she turned up at their house that they agreed to let her come and live with them so she wouldn't have to return home.

For the next eighteen months Marie lived in Florida and found peace for the first time in her life. She loved living in a stable household without violence and hostility, but best of all she liked not having to care for her niece. During that all-too-brief period in Florida, the parents she so despised seemed a million miles away. For the first time in her life she finally felt free.

Everything changed in August 1945, when Jack Lyddy was discharged from Allentown State Hospital and Marie returned home to be with him. She found a job at the DeLong Hook and Eye Company at $25 a week (about $230 today), which she was forced to give her mother toward her keep. Her father was also working as a mechanic at the Brockway Motor Company and for the first time in many years there was regular money coming into the Lyddy household.

Jack started at Gillespie High School but within three months of his release the fifteen-year-old was arrested for larceny. Ella Lyddy was so distressed by her son's arrest, which she saw as a black mark on the family, that she went to court on his behalf as a character witness. She proudly told the judge how her eldest son James had just been honorably discharged from the army after serving overseas and that her daughter Frances had also served her country in the WAACs.

Back in Kensington, Marie was restless and desperate to leave her troubled home. It was like she had never gone to Florida. Once again she longed to escape her parents' bitter arguments but her opportunities were limited, as she was illiterate and could barely write her own name.

Her strange, enigmatic beauty was her only weapon against the world and by this time she had already successfully lured a few neighborhood lads into bed. By the age of nineteen the tall, slender ash-blonde teenager was already sexually experienced beyond her years.

Marie loved flirting and found her sex appeal gave her a real sense of power for the first time. She enjoyed the wolf-whistles and attention she received from workmen as she walked through the drab streets of West Kensington to her new job packing cookies at the Nabisco factory. She craved the attention it brought her and was fast getting a reputation for being "boy-crazy" in her neighborhood.

In early 1948 she began frequenting the Coopersville Singing Club, situated at the corner of Dillman Street and Glenwood Avenue. The private club, in the German section of Kensington, was a popular hang-out for young people who could drink and dance into the early hours.

Most nights Marie put on her best dress and made herself up and went to the club looking for excitement. She would stand at the bar, a drink in one hand, a cigarette in the other, trying to look sophisticated.

One night a desperately shy, pencil-thin young man named Arthur Noe nervously walked up and asked for a dance. She immediately accepted and although the twenty-seven-year-old machinist kept fumbling his steps and chattering incessantly, Marie found him charming and worldly.

When the club closed Arthur walked her home and then asked her out on a date the following night. Marie was delighted, feeling that she had finally found a kindred spirit. That night she slept peacefully for the first time since her return from Florida.

THREE

MARIE AND ARTHUR

Arthur Allen Noe was born on July 18, 1921, into a world he could never come to terms with. The second son of Charles and Elizabeth Noe, a deeply devout Catholic couple from Kensington, his brother Charles was two years older and Arthur was always in his shadow. Times were so hard for the Noes that the brothers had to be placed in St. Vincent's Orphanage as infants until their parents could afford to feed and clothe them.

Growing up, Arthur was a puny, runtish boy who found meager emotional support from his parents. Instead he looked to his stronger elder brother for love and affection. All through his childhood Arthur felt inferior and was bullied mercilessly by the neighborhood boys who nicknamed him Otts, because of his German ancestry. Indeed little Arthur was so desperate to be socially accepted that he would bribe the other children with candy and toys to let him join in their street games.

Every Sunday the Noe family would put on their best clothes to go to Catholic Mass. Arthur loved the pomp and ceremony that seemed worlds removed from the bleak, sooty streets he lived in.

The Noes were poor even by Kensington standards. His more adventurous brother Charles got in with a bad crowd who rustled sheep from a nearby abattoir for extra pocket money. But in April 1928, Charles and his friends were caught in the act of slaughtering a sheep with a long kitchen knife and arrested. The owner told police that rustlers had stolen one hundred and fifty sheep in the previous few months but the boys were let go with a stiff warning after their parents paid compensation for the dead sheep.

As a teenager Arthur seemed a lost soul with few social skills and little direction. A bright boy, he realized that all he could look forward to was spending the rest of his life doing menial work in a local factory. And his growing frustrations could turn violent at the least provocation. He soon developed a reputation in the neighborhood for a vicious temper that could explode at any perceived slight.

"He would become livid with rage and lash out at people," said Linda Harris, a friend and neighbor who was close to Arthur for many years.

After just two years in Northeast Public High School, Arthur decided to drop out and took a job as a floorhand at the Franklin Process cotton factory near his home. When America entered the Second World War, he was ordered to report to the Philadelphia army recruiting office to serve his country. But once again he failed to measure up and was heartbroken when he was classified as 4–F and rejected as physically unfit for the military. Weighing less than a hundred pounds the emaciated teenager already had a chronic history of ulcers caused by bad nerves.

The rejection was a terrible blow to Arthur, who felt even more inadequate than before as he watched his friends leaving Kensington to sail to Europe.

Painfully shy with the opposite sex, and never having had a girlfriend, Arthur became obsessed with losing his virginity during his early twenties. He turned to drink as a necessary tool to make up for the courage he lacked in approaching women. Every night after work he would go to the Coopersville Singing Club, where he devoted himself to trying to find a girlfriend. But his emaciated looks and nervous disposition did not prove popular with the local girls and he always went home alone, feeling more inadequate than ever.

When Linda Harris, which is not her real name, first met Arthur in his early twenties she felt sorry for him and became his confidante. He would spend hours complaining to her that he couldn't get a girl, asking what was wrong with him. Years later she would recall Arthur as a "pathetic little man" who was "always bemoaning the fact that he couldn't get a girl interested in him."

Everything changed one Saturday night in early 1948 when nineteen-year-old Marie Lyddy walked into the Coopersville Club. Arthur was immediately taken by the slender blue-eyed blonde although she was a head taller than he was, and overcame his shyness to go over and ask for a dance.

For the rest of the evening Arthur chattered nervously as Marie sat and listened, saying little. And as the night drew on and the beers kept coming, Arthur fell in love. He could hardly believe his good fortune at finally discovering a pretty girl who liked him.

When the club closed at 3:00 a.m. Arthur gallantly insisted on walking Marie home and when he asked her out again she accepted without hesitation.

For their first date they returned to the club and Arthur declared his undying love as Marie simply smiled enigmatically. Later she willingly responded to his clumsy romantic advances and by the end of the evening they were courting.

The following week Arthur arrived at her front door with a bouquet of flowers. Then he surprised Marie by going down on one knee to propose marriage. Marie immediately accepted, seeing her shy twenty-seven-year-old suitor as the perfect escape from her parents.

"It was a whirlwind courtship," explained Linda Harris. "He was overwhelmed by Marie."

But when Marie came home and told her father that she was engaged he was furious, forbidding her from ever seeing Arthur again. James Lyddy had always considered his youngest daughter slow-witted, and was concerned that the far older Arthur, whom he presumed to be more worldly, would take advantage of her.

But Marie had made up her mind and was determined to marry Arthur with or without her parents' permission. When Arthur suggested that they elope, she immediately packed an overnight case and left her embittered home forever.

On June 1, 1948, Marie and Arthur took a Greyhound bus to Millbourne, Pennsylvania, where they were married before a justice of the peace in a civil ceremony. The sun shone down on a crystal clear early summer day that seemed infinitely full of promise, as they caught the next bus back to Philadelphia to begin a new life together.

The newlyweds were unable to afford their own place, so they moved in with Arthur's parents at 240 W. Atlantic. But there was immediate friction between Marie and Elizabeth Noe, who also did not approve of her son's choice of bride. Right from the very beginning,

Elizabeth constantly complained to neighbors about her new daughter-in-law's failings as a housekeeper. She made no effort to hide her intense dislike for Marie, who she never felt was good enough for her youngest son. The two women in Arthur's life would never learn to like each other.

When James Lyddy heard that his daughter had disobeyed him, he was furious. But being realistic, he agreed to meet his new son-in-law for a man-to-man talk a few days after the couple returned from Pennsylvania.

"My father never wanted Marie to be married and I can understand why," said Marie's sister Anne. "But after they eloped and married my father and Art—that's what we call him—had an agreement that he would be a good husband."

Although he himself was a high-school drop-out, Arthur had always considered himself well-educated with a fine vocabulary. He loved introducing long words into his everyday conversation at any opportunity, feeling it made him seem intelligent.

Arthur was appalled that Marie could barely write her name or do simple sums. As they settled down to married life, Arthur decided to try and educate his illiterate new bride. He insisted that she spend time each day studying the dictionary and learning simple math tables from old textbooks, under his tutelage.

"I understood I had a disadvantage," Marie would later explain. "It took me quite a while to understand . . . words, especially if it was a long word." Eventually Marie learned to read tabloid newspapers and simple books, but she would always appear mentally slow to everyone around her. "She got me, and *I* taught her," Arthur would boast many years later. "That was it."

Delighted to have found a wife who appeared to dote on his every word, Arthur now looked forward to having a family of his own to compensate for his own deprived childhood. And just a few weeks after their marriage he was overjoyed when Marie announced she was pregnant.

That Christmas, Marie brought Arthur to officially meet her family at a party at her parents' home. During a turkey dinner, the beaming father-to-be proudly rose from the table to announce that they were going to have a baby. For once Marie displayed some emotion as she accepted congratulations from her enthusiastic brothers and sisters, though James and Ella Lyddy seemed slightly less enthusiastic about her becoming a mother.

Marie loved being the center of attention as she disclosed plans to buy their own apartment once the baby was born. She even asked her sisters if they could throw her a baby shower.

But behind closed doors the Noes' marriage had gotten off to a rocky start, as Marie soon discovered Arthur's wicked temper. His rages had become worse than ever and he surprised friends by belittling Marie in public if she said something he considered stupid.

Most nights they would go drinking in a taproom and roll home drunk, with Marie urgently demanding sex. She had a bigger sexual appetite than Arthur, who began complaining to friends that she was never satisfied with his lovemaking.

In early 1949, Marie's obsessive need to be the center of attention took a weird new twist as, instead of feigning illness, she began crying *rape*. One night when she was seven months pregnant she went to sleep around midnight as she waited for Arthur to come home from the night shift.

She later told police that she was awakened by a "colored" man with a limp, wearing a leather jacket, who broke in through an open door and brutally raped her. Although she would maintain that she put up a struggle and bit her attacker's ear, her father-in-law, who was asleep upstairs, never heard a thing.

When Arthur arrived home from work to find Marie in a state of panic he ran into a corner bar, screaming for the police, saying that his wife had been raped. Marie was then taken to nearby Temple University Hospital for treatment but the police never made an arrest.

"[It] was a terrible thing and it shook Marie up pretty bad," her sister Frances would remember almost twenty years later.

The alleged rape made the Philadelphia *Evening Bulletin* but no one in the neighborhood seriously believed Marie, who would subtly change her story many times over the next few years. They regarded it as yet another ploy to call attention to herself.

Two weeks later Marie Noe returned to Temple University Hospital to give birth to a healthy seven-pound eleven-ounce baby boy named Richard Allen. She was in labor for twelve hours and her baby suffered slight abrasions to his knees during delivery. But otherwise Richard Allen was fine and nurses congratulated the couple on a beautiful new son.

Arthur Noe was delighted to be a father and proudly took Polaroid photos of Marie holding their angelic new baby to show his factory coworkers. He also took out a

$100 Prudential life insurance policy on his new son the day he was born.

But twenty-year-old Marie seemed melancholic and strangely indifferent to motherhood. The hospital nurses were surprised when she refused to feed her new son after his birth. They noted that Arthur seemed far more comfortable holding the new baby than Marie, who seemed rather numb to it all.

Five days later Richard Allen was discharged from the hospital with a slight case of jaundice and a rash. Doctors reassured Arthur and Marie that this was perfectly normal, but back at her in-laws on W. Atlantic Street, Marie became convinced there was something wrong with her baby.

"He was very sickly," she would remember many years later. "He was throwing up and he had loose bowels."

Over the next few days when the baby failed to gain weight, Marie called her sister Frances in desperation. Frances, who had lost a child of her own five years earlier, came over and agreed that he looked ill. She thought baby Richard might have colic.

A few days later Marie became alarmed when the baby vomited and took him back to Temple Hospital. When doctors told her that he didn't need treatment and there was nothing to worry about, Marie grudgingly took him home again.

Each afternoon Arthur Noe would kiss his new son good-bye and go off to work, leaving Marie to cope with the baby alone. She began to hate Richard's incessant crying and when she told him to stop he bawled even louder.

A couple of days later Marie couldn't stand it any

more and took Richard the few blocks to St. Christopher's Hospital for Children at Fourth and Lehigh Avenue. This time the doctors kept him in the hospital for two weeks for "colic," before discharging him. Once again they reassured the Noes that there was absolutely nothing to worry about.

But Marie felt a growing sense of anger and resentment at her baby's crying. She longed for Arthur to come home and feed Richard and change his diapers, and relieve her of the responsibility. During the long hours he was away, she would pace up and down the living room, getting more and more agitated and angry.

"He couldn't tell me what was bothering him," she would later say. "He just kept crying."

On April 7th, one day after his discharge from St. Christopher's Hospital, Richard was exactly one month old. It had been a nightmare for Marie, who had become depressed and despondent about being a mother. She felt totally overwhelmed by her situation and resolved to change it. Increasingly she felt a strange compulsion to silence his crying once and for all.

Although she knew it was wrong to hurt a baby, these strange, unnatural urges began to engulf her. They were so seductive and irresistible—and they were getting stronger and stronger.

That Thursday night Arthur was working his 3:00 p.m. to midnight shift, leaving Marie alone in the house. At about 9:00 p.m. she began preparing Richard for bed. She bathed and dressed him in his night clothes, placing him on his back in his bassinet at the end of the bed.

As she tip-toed out of the room he began crying louder than ever. Richard's high-pitched wails seemed to drill into Marie's head and she could no longer control herself. Never feeling any real love or connection to the baby, she now saw him as an enemy, sapping the life out of her.

Taking a deep breath, she picked him up and turned him over on his belly, face-down into the pillow. Placing her hand over the back of his head, she used all her strength to drive his tiny face into the soft bedding as she waited for him to die. Finally, a couple of minutes later, he was completely still and she relaxed her grip and let him go.

Stepping back from the bed she looked at her dead baby and a strange peace came over her. For the first time since his birth Marie felt whole again. She lay down on her bed next to him and fell asleep, waiting for her husband to come home.

Shortly after midnight Arthur Noe returned and went straight upstairs to the bedroom. When he picked up the baby he was horrified to find him cold, telling Marie that something was wrong. Rubbing the sleep from her eyes Marie thought fast. She told her husband that when she last looked a minute ago the baby had been sound asleep.

Then Arthur went into shock. Shrouding his son's lifeless body in a blanket, he ran next door to a neighbor, who drove them to Episcopal Hospital where Richard was declared dead on arrival.

"They did what they could but they could not revive him," Marie would say later. "They came out and told us he was dead."

Two days later Richard Allen Noe was buried at the Greenwood Knights of Pythias Cemetery in a $162 funeral arranged by the Charles J. Roman Funeral Home.

It was paid for out of the insurance policy his father had taken on his life.

As there were no grounds for suspicion, an autopsy was not performed. The official cause of death was listed as "Congestive heart failure, due to subacute endocarditis," a condition highly unusual in young babies. Strangely, on the death certificate, his Roman Catholic parents had listed his religion as Protestant.

At the family funeral Marie was dressed in black from head to toe and appeared inconsolable, crying throughout the ceremony. Friends and family all felt sorry for the bereaved young parents who had lost their first baby so tragically. But some people noted that Marie's blank stoicism had now been replaced by a new zest for life. She seemed almost cheerful as she thanked everyone for attending her baby's funeral.

Two weeks after the funeral Marie and Arthur were watching television at 8:30 p.m. on a Monday evening when Marie suddenly went blind. The day before she had temporarily lost her sight for a few minutes, but this time, when it didn't return, she was petrified. For the rest of the night Arthur tried his best to comfort her as she repeatedly lapsed into hysterics.

"Marie went into shock," said her sister Anne. "She was blind. Then she became mute."

The following morning Arthur Noe led Marie into Episcopal Hospital where she was examined by a Dr. Rodgers, who diagnosed her as probably suffering from "an acute conversion hysteria" and ordered a complete psychological evaluation.

Later that day consultant psychologist Dr. N. G. Shaffritz put Marie under the "truth drug," sodium amytal, and questioned her about the state of her marriage and her recent loss. Although he found her friendly and co-operative he noted that the pretty teenager was "some-what on guard," failing to mention the brief bouts of blindness she had experienced regularly since her first period.

During the two-hour session with Dr. Shaffritz, Marie confided that she had deliberately concealed her true feelings since her baby's death. She added that she was also very worried about a favorite uncle who was dangerously ill. She told the doctor that the uncle had been "a second father" to her and she was far closer to him than her own father, whom she described as "very stupid."

When asked how she had reacted to her baby's death, Marie explained that she had discussed it with her husband and both had decided it had been unavoidable. She told him she didn't blame herself or anyone else for his death.

"Both parents seem greatly disturbed," wrote Dr. Shaffritz in his report, carefully noting that Marie showed "inadequate personality development."

He also found that Marie blamed Arthur for her blindness, saying that he had flown into a rage the night it happened, refusing to "permit" her to have another child after she had said she wanted one. She also complained that the marriage had been under great strain since, as she was post-partum, her family doctor had forbidden sex until further notice. She told the doctor that the only thing preventing her from leaving Arthur was money.

"She feels like a stranger with her husband," wrote Dr. Shaffritz.

Dr. Shaffritz diagnosed Marie's blindness as a "hysterical conversion case" but felt that Marie should be able to get better if and when Arthur allowed her to have another child.

At 3:00 p.m., three-and-a-half hours after first being admitted to Episcopal Hospital, Marie suddenly regained her sight and was released the following day.

Marie soon settled back into life with her in-laws. The Noes all seemed to be sympathetic about her recent loss with the exception of her mother-in-law, who told friends that she didn't consider Marie a good mother. Marie began to think that Elizabeth now suspected her of something and deliberately found a job at a nearby ribbon factory so she could escape her mother-in-law's constant disapproving looks.

Over the next few weeks Marie begged Arthur to allow her to have another baby, placing their marriage under increasing pressure. Every night she tried to seduce him when they returned from the taproom. At first he tried to resist her, saying it was against doctor's orders, but eventually he gave in and by the beginning of 1950 Marie was pregnant again.

FOUR

LIFE WITH THE NOES

At the dawn of the 1950s there was an exodus of young people leaving Kensington. The Second World War had broadened the horizons of many young Kensington men who had served abroad, discovering a world outside their home town. Some had returned with war brides, who wanted to move away from the sooty, grimy factory streets to the suburbs, which were far more suitable for raising children.

The GI Bill of Rights, which paid veterans to go to college, saw other ambitious young men start commuting to Temple and Villanova Colleges. And after graduating they decided that parochial Kensington offered little opportunity for advancement in the world.

But others like Arthur and Marie Noe had little choice in the matter and could not afford to move even if they had wanted to.

"This was a real old-style neighborhood in the full sense of the word," explained social historian Vince Ziemba, who grew up on the borders in Richmond. "Everybody knew each other from the stoops and there was a real community spirit here."

The Noes blended in well in the drab Cooperstown section of Kensington. Although they were considered good neighbors the tall, blonde-haired Marie had acquired a "bad" reputation and was the subject of much gossip.

"It was no secret in the neighborhood that Marie was seeing other men on the side," Linda Harris would later tell an investigator from the Philadelphia Medical Examiner's Office. "She had always been considered boy-crazy."

Marie had developed a crush on a young married neighbor named Robert Valentine, whom she had known since her childhood. It was common knowledge that Marie was "wildly in love" with the handsome young man, but it was unrequited, as he considered her "childish."

Many years later she would admit to having at least one affair with a local man after meeting him in a taproom. But afterwards she felt so guilty that she owned up to a furious Arthur, who insisted she be examined by a doctor for sexually transmitted diseases before he forgave her.

Although Arthur was only too aware of Marie's indiscretions he stayed loyal, insisting to friends she was a good wife and never played around. But at home they would have furious arguments about the increasing attentions she paid other men.

During the last trimester of her second pregnancy Marie was rushed to hospital on four separate occasions with false labor. Each time Arthur, who had prudently taken out Blue Cross medical coverage, drove her to the hospital and then back again.

Finally on September 8th, 1950, Marie gave birth to a healthy seven-pound ten-ounce baby girl named Elizabeth Mary. Within hours of her birth Arthur called his broker and took out a $100 life insurance policy on his new daughter.

Although the doctors declared Elizabeth to be in perfect health when her parents took her home to W. Atlantic Street, things soon started to go wrong. After the birth Marie returned to her job at the ribbon factory, leaving her mother-in-law to look after the granddaughter who bore her name. But eventually Marie found working full-time and being a mother too strenuous and quit her job to stay home.

At first Elizabeth seemed to thrive, putting on weight and growing rapidly. Each morning Marie would place her in her carriage and show her off to her W. Atlantic Street neighbors. She appeared to delight in the compliments she received on her beautiful new baby, who always looked well-dressed and appeared well taken care of.

"Elizabeth was pretty good until she got a cold," Marie would recall many years later. "Then she got cranky."

In January 1951, Marie rushed her to her family doctor with a temperature of 105 degrees. The doctor was not unduly worried, as Elizabeth reacted well to medicine and the fever soon subsided.

Although Elizabeth had gained a full ten pounds since birth and appeared perfectly healthy, her mother seemed strangely distracted and withdrawn. Again she felt almost compelled to harm her baby and become a person in her own right again.

Three weeks later on Saturday, February 17, Marie Noe was home alone with Elizabeth, who was lying in her bassinet in the dining room. Suddenly the baby started crying and all Marie's feelings of anger and resentment bubbled to the surface. Turning the tiny baby over on her back, she took a pillow from the bed and placed it over her face and began to suffocate her.

"She was fussing," would be Marie's simple explanation during her later confession.

But the five-month nine-day-old baby was far bigger and stronger than her younger brother had been and put up a desperate fight for life. It took all Marie's strength to smother the last breath out of her tiny daughter.

"I held the pillow over her face until she stopped moving," she would later state without a flicker of emotion.

Satisfied that her baby was dead, Marie then went in to the living room to wait for Elizabeth's body to be discovered.

Thirty minutes later her brother-in-law Charles walked in and found the baby turning blue. He began shouting for help and Marie came rushing into the dining room and straight over to Elizabeth. She registered no emotion as she touched the baby and pronounced it cold, telling Charles to call the police. Within minutes the rescue squad arrived and after a cursory examination said it was too late to save the baby.

Marie Noe's explanation to the police dispatchers was that she had brought Elizabeth downstairs from her bedroom and given her a bottle. After leaving the dining room she had returned to discover her baby in her crib, "vomiting milk mixed with blood."

Elizabeth Noe was officially declared dead on arrival at Temple Hospital. The coroner held an autopsy, determining the cause of death as bronchopneumonia. It was a condition that could only be proved microscopically, but surprisingly there is no evidence of any internal examination ever being carried out.

As a matter of routine the police opened an investigation, questioning Marie in her hospital bed. But they were satisfied with her explanation and the case was closed. An inquest was held on March 14 but any police reports relating to her death have long since disappeared. It was as if Elizabeth Noe had never existed.

In the early 1950s the Philadelphia Medical Examiner's Office was so primitive that ordinary kitchen knives were standard equipment for autopsies. With hundreds of cases passing through every week, no one paid much attention to one dead baby. As a matter of course, death certificates for infants were regularly signed off as "unknown," as no one could be bothered to waste valuable time in such a busy office. And for Marie Noe the system was a godsend.

"Suffocating a baby is the perfect murder," declares Dr. Dimitri Contostavlos, who a decade later became Philadelphia's assistant medical examiner and is now the medical examiner of Delaware County. "We don't like to admit it but we forensic pathologists cannot detect it. There's no sign. Nothing."

Three days after her death Elizabeth Noe was laid to rest at the Greenwood Cemetery alongside her baby brother. Once again Marie Noe played the part of the distraught mother to perfection, standing by the tiny coffin with Arthur to accept condolences from friends and family. It was, as everyone agreed, a tragedy, but Marie impressed many with her positive attitude, which verged on martyrdom. She would try again for another baby, she declared after the service.

Soon after Elizabeth's death, Marie and Arthur moved into their own three-room apartment at 215 W. Ontario Street. Relations between Marie and Elizabeth Noe had reached the breaking point with her mother-in-law's constant criticism of her abilities as a mother and house-wife. Marie had become increasingly paranoid, fearing that Elizabeth suspected her of harming her children. Eventually she persuaded Arthur that they should move out.

A few months later Marie found that she was pregnant again and Arthur was delighted. He reassured her that everything would be fine and this time the baby would survive. But Marie said she wished she could be as certain.

The Noes' third baby was born on Wednesday, April 23, 1952, at Episcopal Hospital. Jacqueline Noe entered the world weighing a healthy seven pounds two-and-a-half ounces. Hospital staff could not help noting that Marie seemed disinterested in her new daughter, complaining that a duty doctor had attended the birth, instead of her favorite physician who happened to be off-duty.

Five days later Marie surprised nurses again by discharging herself and leaving Jacqueline in the pediatric ward, so she could go home and take care of Arthur, who was ill. It would be a further five days until she saw Jacqueline again, when the baby was sent home in perfect health.

Now, in their new apartment, Marie again felt overwhelmed at having to take care of her baby. She became so stressed that her sister Frances and Linda Harris would often come around to help her out. Unlike her other two babies, Jacqueline Noe never returned to the hospital after she was born and there are no records of any health problems.

But just ten days after coming home, baby Jacqueline breathed her final breath, alone with her mother in the apartment. She was just three weeks old. To this day Marie Noe says she can't remember what happened to Jacqueline. In her 1998 confession Marie admitted that she doesn't know if the baby's death was deliberate or accidental.

Nonetheless it was a beautiful Wednesday afternoon when Marie ran the one block to her parents' house at W. Tioga Street, cradling her dead baby in a blanket. Her sisters Anne and Frances were sitting on the stoop when they heard Marie's screams for help.

"Marie was scared to death," remembers Anne. "Our eldest sister Frances just grabbed the baby as Marie said, 'She's not breathing! She's not breathing!' "

Frances tried unsuccessfully to resuscitate Jacqueline with C.P.R. and then James Lyddy drove them to Episcopal Hospital, where the baby was pronounced dead on arrival.

When police detectives arrived at the hospital shortly afterwards, Marie claimed that she had found her baby turning blue and vomiting, and had wrapped her in a blanket before seeking help. Once again the police accepted her explanation and never returned to question her further.

With the untimely loss of their third child there was a great deal of sympathy for the Noes in Kensington. Several days before the funeral some of their neighbors took up a collection to buy flowers for the grave.

But while they were making the rounds of the district they arrived at a corner taproom to discover Marie and Arthur drinking beer and playing shuffleboard, as if they didn't have a care in the world. It wasn't long before the word was out all over the neighborhood that the

Noes were already living it up, before their baby had even been laid to rest.

"People in the neighborhood didn't like it one bit," said Carrie McDonald, who lived across the road from the Noes at the time.

The coroner ruled the official cause of death as "inspiration [sic] of vomitus" and although an autopsy was performed and an inquest held, all records have long since disappeared.

Jacqueline Noe, who had barely survived three weeks, was buried in a tiny casket at the Greenwood Cemetery as Arthur once again comforted his wife by the graveside.

A few weeks later Marie and Arthur moved a few blocks away to 3452 Rosehill Street to make a fresh start, saying that they hoped it would change their terrible luck. But where once there had been sympathy for the Noes, now many of their neighbors openly questioned whether Marie's babies had died accidentally or if it was something more sinister.

Even Arthur's friend Linda Harris, who had often helped Marie care for her babies, was suspicious. She began to distance herself from the Noes and their friendship would never be the same again.

Soon after Jacqueline's death, Marie asked her obstetrician to tie her tubes so she couldn't have any more babies. The doctor said he was prepared to perform the procedure after her next period, but she would first need her husband's written consent.

While she was waiting she and Arthur sought the spiritual advice of their parish priest at St. Hugh's Church.

"The priest turned around and told her it was God's will," remembered her sister Anne, who wanted her to have the operation. "He said it was a mortal sin and you just take a chance that each child will be born normal. It's a terrible shame and she would never have had these tragedies if she hadn't listened to the priest."

Looking back years later, Marie admitted that she and Arthur had considered using birth control at the time but decided against it for religious reasons.

"I often thought about not getting pregnant again," she told Philadelphia writer Stephen Fried. "Anything not to have to bring another child in the world and [have] another ungodly catastrophe."

Over the next few months Marie's behavior became increasingly bizarre. On one occasion she failed to appear to meet Arthur after work at her new job at Sears–Roebuck. When he went into the store to find his wife he was told that she had already left for the day.

That night Marie failed to return home and Arthur was desperately worried, spending the night scouring the neighborhood for her. The following day he was about to call the police to report her missing when she telephoned collect from Florida, asking him to come and get her. When he asked her what she was doing there, Marie replied that she had gone there with an older man, refusing to elaborate any further.

Furious at his wife's erratic behavior Arthur jumped into his car and drove the 1,500 miles to Florida and found her. But on the journey back to Philadelphia he became so upset that he crashed the car and wrecked it. He would later tell friends that his "intense anger" was to blame.

A few weeks later Marie again failed to come home without a word. But early the next morning she walked through the front door as if nothing was amiss. She calmly told her frantic husband that she had taken a cab to the Y.M.C.A. on W. Allegheny Avenue as she felt her period coming on and became faint. Even though the Y.M.C.A. was a mere four blocks away from their home she had decided to stay the night. Arthur was so relieved to have her home that he immediately forgave her, never bothering to check out her implausible explanation.

Over the next few months Marie began acting more and more strangely. She became convinced that someone was waging a vicious campaign of obscene telephone calls against her and plagued the police with complaints. Some of her friends and neighbors believed she relished the attention, getting an illicit thrill from constantly describing the lurid calls in explicit detail.

Marie also began complaining that strange men were regularly following her home late at night, making Arthur call the police on numerous occasions.

"The police seemed to be at their home all the time," remembered Linda Harris.

Even more macabre were the mysterious deaths of the Noes' pets at their new home on Rosehill Street. Over the two years they lived there an assortment of pet dogs, cats, birds, fish and turtles were all found dead in unexplained circumstances.

Soon after Jacqueline's death, Linda Harris gave the Noes a cocker spaniel as a gift. One day Arthur arrived home and asked Marie what had happened to his pet dog. She calmly replied that she had called the SPCA to have it put to death "because it had the raves."

On another occasion Arthur came home to discover their two parakeets lying dead on the floor of their cage. When he asked his wife what had happened she had no explanation. It now became a common occurrence for Arthur to arrive home from work to find pet cats and dogs lying dead in the cellar.

When a concerned Linda Harris broached the subject of the dead animals, Marie sadly complained, "Everything I touch dies!"

In February 1954, Arthur's brother Charles died after a long illness. In recent years the brothers had become bitter enemies and openly despised each other. Charles's wife had run off with another man several years earlier. He had never gotten over the shock and had sunk into a deep depression.

In August 1954, Marie Noe celebrated her 26th birthday at a family party, where she announced that she and Arthur were trying to have another baby. It was an emotional moment for her family, who would dutifully stand by her through thick and thin.

"It was very difficult for Marie," said her sister Anne, who was closest to her. "She was a very caring person and she always babysitted [sic] for members of the family. We had no problems with her."

But some of her neighbors were not quite as happy about leaving Marie alone with their babies. That August, Linda Harris organized a christening party for her new grandson and invited many old friends from the neighborhood, including the Noes. Everyone knew about Marie's sad history and some parents strongly objected to Marie being left alone with a new-born baby. It was therefore decided before the party that the baby would be closely supervised at all times, just in case.

In the midst of the party Marie suddenly left the rest of the adults to go outside and join some of the younger children who were playing in the garden on swings. It was a beautiful summer afternoon and Marie started gently pushing the swinging children into the air.

At one point Linda Harris' sister happened to look out the kitchen window. She was shocked to see a visibly angry Marie giving one of the three-year-olds such a violent push that he fell off the swing to the ground.

Marie then returned to the party and joined the other adults in the basement where they later retired for drinks.

"The baby was momentarily forgotten," Harris would later tell an investigator. "Suddenly, at one point, someone called out, 'The baby!' "

Everyone rushed upstairs to the nursery where the baby was sleeping in its crib. They entered to find Marie bending over the basinet with her hands up near the baby's throat.

Somebody screamed "Marie!" and she straightened up fast, calmly explaining that she was only arranging the baby's covers. There were many at the party who were far from convinced and felt that the baby had had a narrow escape.

Soon after the christening party Marie claimed she had been raped again. She later told police that she had returned home in the afternoon from her new job at the Paragon Textile Mills, left her handbag on the kitchen table and went upstairs to her bedroom. When she opened up a clothes closet, a tall red-haired man in a leather jacket leapt out at her and she fainted in terror.

On regaining consciousness, Marie found herself under the bed, bound and gagged with several of her husband's brand-new neckties and was unable to escape.

There was no sign of the rapist, who had made off with $15 from her handbag.

Half an hour later Arthur Noe arrived home and could not find his wife. Presuming she was still at work, he sat down to wait for her. Two hours later when she had still not appeared, he decided to go out and search for her. He went up to the bedroom to change out of his work clothes and discovered a hysterical Marie tied up under the bed.

He rushed her to Episcopal hospital where she was treated for shock. But the emergency room report found no signs of any of the physical trauma that would be expected to accompany a savage rape or strangulation.

A brief report of the alleged attack was carried in the *Philadelphia Inquirer* as a police roundup item under the headline "Faints At Seeing Thug."

Police were never able to capture the red-headed attacker in the leather jacket, although some skeptics wondered if there was some other ulterior motive for her story.

FIVE

ONE AFTER THE OTHER

Exactly nine months to the day after her alleged attack, Marie gave birth to a healthy baby boy at Episcopal Hospital on April 23, 1955. The eleven-pound eleven-ounce bouncing baby was named Arthur Jr. after his proud father, although Marie thought he bore a stronger resemblance to Arthur's recently deceased brother Charles.

"[Arthur Jr.] had long dark hair," she would later recall. "It looked like it was going to be curly."

Claiming she didn't want to take any chances and risk losing another baby if her street was blocked, Marie asked a nearby private ambulance service to be on alert in case of emergency. But when the manager demanded $200 up-front to join, she declined.

Five days after Arthur Jr.'s birth the Noes took out a $1,000 Sun Life insurance policy. They also purchased a second policy with The Prudential.

Their fourth baby had only been home five days when his mother rushed him back to Episcopal's accident ward, complaining that he was having difficulty breathing. The doctors couldn't find anything wrong and gave him a clean bill of health before sending him home.

The next day Arthur Jr. was home alone with his mother when he stopped breathing altogether and turned blue. He was just twelve days old when he died.

"I only remember bits and pieces about Arthur dying," Marie would confess more than forty years later. "I don't remember if I did anything to Arthur or not."

This time it was Marie who called the rescue squad and accompanied Arthur Jr. to Episcopal Hospital, where he was pronounced dead on arrival. A regular autopsy was carried out, with the coroner ruling that Arthur Jr. had died of bronchopneumonia.

Several days later Marie donned her black mourning dress yet again to stand arm-in-arm with Arthur as their fourth baby was laid to rest in Greenwood Cemetery, alongside his brother and two sisters. He was smartly dressed in a new set of clothes. The funeral costs were more than covered by baby Arthur's life insurance policies, which were paid out in full within days of his death.

Soon after Arthur Jr.'s death Marie Noe went blind again, just as she had after losing her other three children. But as before, her sight soon returned and the Noes returned to their routine life, trying to put the past behind them.

Every day Arthur and Marie left home for their respective jobs and then spent the evenings in their favorite taproom at the junction of Philip and Tioga Streets, drinking and playing shuffleboard. Whenever kindly neighbors brought up the subject of their dead babies, Arthur and Marie were only too happy to discuss it and bemoan the ungodly tragedy that had befallen them.

Losing four children in such unexplained circumstances had made the Noes a major talking point in Kensington, where everyone knew everyone else's business. But the neighborhood was firmly divided between those who believed the deaths were natural and those who did not.

"Everybody talked about the Noes," remembers their neighbor Alexander Zimba, who was in high school in the mid-1950s. "Everybody had an opinion. Some people would say they thought it was peculiar and others would say it was an act of God."

Once again Arthur Noe tried to reverse their bad luck by moving to a house on 3447 N. American Street, down the road from St. Hugh's Parish Church. Marie found a new job at Arrow Designs on Glenwood Avenue and Arthur continued working as a floorman at the Franklin factory, where he'd been employed for more than a decade.

One day a priest from St. Hugh's arrived at the Noes' new home to welcome them to his parish. But after walking into the front room he was horrified to see Salvador Dali's surrealistic depiction of the crucifixion hanging in their front room. Taking immediate offense, the priest asked the Noes to take it down, saying that it was sacrilegious. Arthur Noe became so incensed that he threw the priest out of his house and immediately resigned from St. Hugh's in protest.

Tortured by the loss of his children, Arthur began drinking heavily and chain-smoking as he desperately tried to make sense out of what had happened. He questioned why he and Marie had been cursed with the loss of so many children, deciding they must have been singled out by God to bear this awful burden.

In the summer of 1957, Marie became pregnant again. It was, she told Arthur, a sign from God. And to celebrate their good fortune they both agreed to return to the Roman Catholic Church to have their marriage officially blessed.

On February 24, 1958, Marie Noe gave birth to a healthy baby girl at St. Luke's Hospital. The Noes named their new seven-pound eight-ounce baby Constance, and although she was born with conjunctivitis it soon cleared up.

Marie had deliberately chosen a new hospital for this birth, saying that she did not wish to be reminded of what had happened in the past. Therefore the St. Luke's doctors, who had never treated her before, were unaware of her tragic medical history. Soon after Constance's birth her obstetrician, Dr. Spengler, who had performed the delivery, asked a young pediatrician named Dr. Abraham Perlman to look in on the mother and her new baby.

Dr. Perlman first met Marie Noe during a routine examination in the maternity ward when Constance was just a day old and still unnamed. He knew nothing about the untimely deaths of her other four babies. After cheerfully introducing himself, Dr. Perlman explained that he would be supervising her pediatric care and then complimented her on having such a beautiful baby.

"What's the use!" said Marie forlornly to the astonished pediatrician. "She's going to die just like all the others."

Dr. Perlman was so shocked by Marie's pessimistic reaction, which he had never before encountered in a mother, that he immediately requested her records and discovered her dark medical history.

"After that it stopped being routine," Dr. Perlman would tell police in 1998. "I examined the baby more often than normal and I ordered more studies than I normally do."

Determined to leave nothing to chance, he ordered every conceivable test for Constance, including X-rays, special blood tests and even one for syphilis. But everything came back negative.

When Dr. Perlman told Marie Noe that Constance was perfectly healthy she again informed him that it wouldn't make any difference as the baby wouldn't make it. The doctor was horrified by Marie's strange indifference to her baby and would never forget the encounter.

During Marie's week-long stay in the maternity ward, Dr. Perlman examined Constance every day, giving her special attention. When Constance was discharged in good condition, a beaming Arthur Noe arrived to drive his wife and new daughter home to N. American Street.

Two weeks later on March 19th—two days after Arthur Noe took out a life insurance policy on Constance— Marie Noe called her family doctor, saying that the baby was not breathing properly. After examining Constance at home and diagnosing a common cold, which wasn't responding to medication, he had the baby re-admitted to St. Luke's for blood tests to be on the safe side.

The ambulance arrived and first mistakenly brought Marie and Constance to the first aid room at Temple Hospital before proceeding on to St. Luke's. For the next three days Constance was given a battery of tests and kept under close observation before she was allowed to go home the following Saturday afternoon.

The next day Arthur took his wife and new baby daughter on a drive to the country, feeling that they had finally changed their luck and everything would work out fine.

"The car was warm enough," Arthur later told a reporter. "[Constance] seemed healthy—a beautiful baby."

The following evening Arthur Noe left work and went to St. Hugh's Church for religious instruction in preparation for his impending marital blessing. Afterward he went drinking in his favorite taproom.

Back alone at N. American Street with Constance, Marie decided to celebrate her baby's one-month anniversary by training her to sit up in a chair. Placing the tiny baby on a chair in the parlor, she arranged one pillow behind her and set another chair in front to support her so she wouldn't topple over. Suddenly Constance began to cry and Marie lost control.

"I don't know why," she would later confess. "but then I took a pillow and laid her down on the chair and I suffocated her."

Then in a dream-like state Marie carefully carried Constance to her crib and closed her eyes as if she were asleep. Then she left the room and went upstairs to the bathroom to compose herself. There she remained until she heard her husband come through the front door.

Arthur Noe walked into the parlor to see his baby daughter lying dead in her pink basinet. In shocked desperation he tried to resuscitate her, but to his horror, as he pressed down on the baby's abdomen, milk curds came out of her nose and mouth.

He immediately telephoned the rescue squad and then ran next door to his neighbor, Violetta Zimba, asking if she knew anything about artificial respiration.

"He said he had just come home from the taproom

or the club and found the baby turning blue in the bassinet," she later told the police.

When Violetta walked into the Noe parlor she saw Marie standing by her dead baby, wringing her hands in anguish. The lifeless baby was still warm but there were no signs of life whatsoever.

"As soon as I [saw the baby] I knew it needed a doctor," remembered Violetta Zimba. "I said, 'Marie, you better call a doctor and get some help. Get down to the hospital as fast as you can!' "

Rooted to the spot, Marie remained as still as a statue, not appearing to comprehend what was happening. As Violetta and Arthur desperately tried to resuscitate Constance, she stood wringing her hands and moaning in grief.

Finally the rescue squad arrived and the firemen placed the baby's arms behind her back and put an oxygen mask over her tiny face. They wrapped her in a blanket and carried her out to an emergency vehicle for the short trip to Episcopal Hospital. Throughout, Marie Noe seemed oblivious to the activity around her and strangely preoccupied. Eventually she came to and told Arthur to accompany Constance to the hospital.

A short time later Marie was driven to the hospital by Violetta's husband, but by the time she arrived Constance had already been pronounced dead. Marie was asked to sit in the waiting room with Arthur so they could be questioned by detectives.

"When the detectives got there they asked us an awful lot of questions," recalled Marie. "And they even came back to our house and looked around."

During the next few hours police detectives and investigators from the office of the medical examiner scoured the Noe's two-storey row house, looking for any clues to explain Constance's death. They removed bottles of milk, water and various food items to test and questioned Marie about what had happened.

When asked many years later if she had ever feared being caught killing her babies, Marie Noe answered candidly: "I was hoping they would. I knew what I was doing was very wrong."

The following day *Evening Bulletin* reporter Dick Bowman arrived at the Noes' house to interview them about the death of their fifth baby. He found the parents in mourning but unusually cooperative and only too willing to discuss their recent loss.

"The tall, thin, brown-haired woman scanned the living room with gaunt eyes," started the story which ran the following day.

"She stroked the ears of her two dogs, Tiny and Spot. 'This is the only family we seem able to keep,' she said softly.

"For Mary [sic] Noe, 29, the death of her fifth child was too much for tears. For husband Arthur, 37, a short wiry man, his new found religious faith was getting the acid test."

The Noes proudly showed Bowman around their house, pointing out Constance's tiny pink bassinet. At one point in the interview Marie suddenly announced that she was going back to work there and then, adding: "I don't have anything better to do."

Close to tears, Arthur told Bowman about the deaths of his five children, showing the reporter their pictures from a photo album.

"People keep asking us why our children can't seem

to live," he said, twisting his thin, bony hands. "Only God knows the answer, I guess.

"We moved every time Mary [sic] was pregnant. Tried to change our luck. But fate seemed to dog us. We couldn't escape it. We gave our children all we could. I'm not rich, but we did our best."

After the funeral Marie remained by her daughter's grave long after the other mourners had departed. Her parents waited with her, trying to coax her to leave, but she appeared to be in her own world.

"It seemed like she couldn't stand to go home," her mother Ella Lyddy would later say. "She was just all filled up."

SIX

SUFFER THE LITTLE CHILDREN

A few months before Arthur Jr.'s death the Philadelphia Medical Examiner's Office had been transformed—some might say dragged into the twentieth century—by the arrival of Dr. Joseph Spelman from the ME's office in Vermont. Dr. Spelman recruited a crack team of pathologists and investigators and updated the office with state-of-the-art equipment.

"He was one of the early major players in establishing quality medical legal death investigation in this country," said Dr. Robert Catherman, who would work under Spelman in the late 1960s, "and when he came to Philadelphia he took a special interest in these crib deaths."

In early 1958 a vivacious young pathologist named Dr. Molly Valdes-Dapena walked into Dr. Spelman's office with an unusual request. She wanted to come in twice a week to perform autopsies on the steady stream of dead babies that regularly turned up in his morgue. Spelman gladly accepted her offer. He and his colleagues were already overworked and besides, few pathologists enjoyed dissecting the bodies of babies.

At that time 36-year-old Molly Dapena was a general pathologist at Philadelphia General Hospital, but had recently decided to specialize in baby death.

"I wanted to grow up to be a pediatric pathologist," she explained. "As the youngest and smallest pathology resident in a busy place I got to do the baby autopsies. Nobody else cared about them. Nobody came to see them. In those days it was considered that a baby got born and either lived or died. You didn't do anything. I mean nothing."

Hailing from rural Pottsville, Pennsylvania, Molly Dapena had put herself through medical school before falling for a handsome Cuban man. As he was a pathologist, Molly decided to become one too.

By 1958 Molly had seven children of her own—she would have a further four—and felt a personal commitment to discovering why up to fifteen thousand babies died in unexplained circumstances every year in the United States.

"This was at the time of the baby boom," she said, "and a lot of babies died and I did a lot of autopsies. I soon discovered that nobody knew a lot about it or even what was normal. And that remains the case to this day."

Soon after she arrived at the Philadelphia Medical Examiner's Office, Dr. Spelman asked her to conduct an autopsy on the body of Constance Noe in late March 1958. Although the initial on-scene diagnosis had been "aspiration of vomitus" due to natural or accidental causes, Dr. Dapena remained unconvinced.

And when the fifth dead Noe baby had arrived at the morgue, Dr. Spelman, who already had his own suspicions about the family, decided to postpone entering the cause of death for forty-five days, until he and the police could carry out a thorough investigation.

During her autopsy on Constance, Dr. Dapena decided that inhalation of vomit was not the direct cause of death. She thought it more likely to be the end result of it and ordered toxicology and microscopic tissue tests. But all the results came back negative.

Remembered Dr. Dapena: "I went to Dr. Spelman and I said, 'Here you are, sir. I just performed this autopsy and I didn't find anything,' and gave him the slides. But of course by this time he already had a series in his hand [from the other Noe babies] and he was the officer of the law. And so from here on it was his ball."

Over the next few weeks Spelman's investigators closely questioned Marie and Arthur Noe about their family medical history, seeking any clues to explain the deaths. A subsequent report from the Office of the Medical Examiner (OME) described Marie as being slow in answering questions and constantly having to rely on her husband's help. It concluded that she "appeared either hyperthyroid or under par mentally."

After the investigation was completed Dr. Spelman met with Dr. Dapena to discuss the results and their implications. With no scientific answers to explain Constance's death, they agreed to register the official cause of death as "Undetermined, Presumed Natural."

That same week the Sun Life Insurance Company paid out $1,250 on the policy Arthur had taken out on Constance Noe. A few months later Marie and Arthur would go shopping and buy a new living room suite for $1,200.

In early 1959 Arthur and Marie's families gathered in St. Hugh's Church to witness them renew their marriage vows and have their union officially blessed by the Catholic Church. The years had not been kind to Marie, who had a haunted look in her eyes and was white as a sheet. Again pregnant, she shuffled up the aisle as though she had the cares of the world on her broad shoulders. Although well-dressed in a cream suit, her once-beautiful blonde hair was now a greasy brown and unwashed.

As the guests watched the oddly matched couple exchange vows, it was difficult to believe that Marie had just turned thirty and her rail-thin husband was only thirty-six. They both appeared to be at least twenty years older.

Once again Marie took center stage, telling friends and relatives how this renewal of their marriage vows in church marked a new start. There was little talk about their upcoming baby; Marie's growing belly made everyone slightly uncomfortable.

As Marie Noe prepared for her sixth child, Arthur's aged parents moved in with their son and daughter-in-law, along with Marie's troubled younger brother John, who was homeless at the time. Two years earlier Charles Noe, now in his mid-eighties, had retired and a few weeks, later in the spring of 1957, seventy-five-year-old Elizabeth Noe was laid off from her cleaning job. As the aged couple could no longer support themselves, they moved their meager possessions into 3447 N. American Street so Elizabeth could help Marie take care of her new baby.

Before long the two women were at loggerheads again. Marie was scared of Elizabeth and felt her mother-in-law still suspected that she had killed her babies. She began trying to turn Arthur against his mother by telling him that the old woman was senile and therefore mentally suspect.

On August 24, 1959, Marie's sixth baby, Letitia, was stillborn at thirty-nine weeks at St. Luke's Hospital. The fetus had been so active in the womb that the umbilical cord had become knotted, cutting off the flow of blood and oxygen to the mother. Marie and Arthur decided to donate Letitia's body to the hospital for medical research.

1960 was a watershed year for America. John F. Kennedy squeaked through to victory over Richard Nixon by a mere 118,000 votes and as a new decade dawned a fresh wind of change blew through the country, bringing with it a new optimism.

Arthur Noe was delighted at the Kennedy victory. A lifelong Democrat, he began to involve himself in Kensington politics, working for Democratic ward leader and later councilman Harry Janotti, whom he regarded as one of the finest men who had ever lived. Over the next few years Arthur would become one of Janotti's most loyal supporters, often going house-to-house to campaign for him at election time.

Arthur loved being a small cog in the powerful Democratic political machine. He felt it gave him real respectability and a new importance in the neighborhood.

On May 17, 1960, Marie Noe began a new job in the packing and finishing department of the Display Corp. of America on Stenton Avenue, but was let go three weeks later. She resumed work there in July but was again laid off in mid-September, returning two weeks later.

The following year Arthur Noe, who had left his job at the Franklin Process to take up a new position in the Bundy and Coleman factory, found himself in the need of a job when his employers went out of business. Using his political connections he soon found work as a warehouseman at Zurn Industries on Sedgely Avenue, taking home $303 every month after taxes.

Then in late April 1962, Marie Noe became pregnant again and took a leave of absence from her job to prepare for the birth of her seventh baby. She found a new family physician, Dr. Columbus Gangemi, on Foulkrod Street, Kensington, who was intrigued to hear about her tragic medical history. Throughout her pregnancy she would regularly visit his office to discuss her medical problems and the various fears she felt about having another child.

Mary Lee Noe was born one month prematurely by cesarean section on June 19, 1962, at St. Joseph's Hospital, weighing six pounds, eight ounces. During the difficult delivery Marie suffered severe vascular collapse and anemia.

Dr. Gangemi and Marie's new obstetrician, Dr. Salvatore Cucinotta, had both advised her to have the baby in St. Joseph's Hospital across the city, where the baby remained under close observation for a month to ensure that everything was all right.

Marie would later claim that the doctors did not expect Mary Lee to survive, as she had a respiratory problem and was put in an oxygen tent and given an IV drip. "It was several hours until I knew she was going to be all right," she remembered.

After Mary Lee was discharged in mid-July, Marie Noe began calling Dr. Gangemi as often as five times a day to discuss the baby. Dr. Gangemi found his new patient to be "highly nervous and excitable," but surprisingly unemotional about the deaths of her children. "She would complain that the baby cried all the time and was getting on her nerves," he would later explain.

"and that she couldn't take all that crying constantly."

Her obstetrician Dr. Cucinotta now claims he doubted Marie's sanity from the very beginning, urging Dr. Gangemi to take some action. "She was a blank person," said Dr. Cucinotta in 1998. "I wanted to send her to a psychiatrist but her family doctor refused."

During Mary Lee's short life, Linda Harris formed a great attachment to the beautiful little girl. She made frequent visits to N. American Street to feed and dress the plump, blue-eyed baby, finding her a "picture of health and very bright."

When Mary Lee was six weeks old, Arthur took out a $1,250 life insurance policy on her with Sun Life and another one on Marie two months later. He also took out three separate life insurance policies on his ailing mother for a total of $405 with the Prudential. In October Elizabeth Noe fell ill and entered St. Luke's Hospital where she spent three weeks before being discharged.

That Christmas, Mary Lee became only the second Noe baby to live through the festive season. Plunging himself into the Christmas spirit, Arthur bought a tree for the front room and invited the family over for the trimming ceremony, where he constantly fussed over his new daughter as he opened her gifts for her.

On Friday, December 28, Marie took Mary Lee, now six months old and weighing a healthy twenty pounds, to Dr. Gangemi for her last weekly visit of the year.

"She got a needle and the doctor looked her [over] pretty thoroughly," Marie would later recall. "He was satisfied with the way she was."

One week later on January 4, 1963, Marie Noe woke up at 6:30 a.m. to get her husband ready for work. After he left the house at 8:00 a.m. she took Mary Lee upstairs to bathe her.

"My husband's parents were downstairs arguing as usual," she later told police. "I bathed the baby and dressed her and brought her downstairs and tried to get her to take a bottle. She refused.

"She was acting very nervous and upset from the quarreling and I didn't know what to do so I took her to my mother's house."

While at her mother's, two blocks away on W. Tioga Street, the baby calmed down and even took a two-hour nap. At 10:30 a.m. Marie took her home again, where Mary Lee became "cranky and fussy." Hoping to quiet her down, Marie took her upstairs, but as she was "still fussy," rocked her to sleep.

A few minutes later Mary Lee woke up and started crying. Marie went downstairs to get a bottle and fed the baby, who drank the milk and promptly fell asleep.

In her 1998 confession Marie Noe claimed to no longer remember anything about the day Mary Lee died or if she had harmed her, though on the day it happened she gave police the following detailed explanation:

"I left the room for a few minutes and when I came back she was gasping for breath and turning blue. So I called the telephone operator and told her and she connected me with the police. They told me they would send someone right over to help me."

Then she called Arthur at work with the dreadful news and he rushed straight home, arriving just before the police and the rescue squad, who unsuccessfully tried to revive Mary Lee with oxygen.

"I tried to give the baby mouth-to-mouth respiration," Marie would claim. "Then the police got there."

Police Officer William White, who was assigned to Philadelphia's 25th District, was sent to the Noes' house by his radio dispatcher. He rushed up to the first floor where he saw rescue workers desperately working on Mary Lee.

"The mother seemed to be in a daze, like a zombie," he would later remember. "Someone said, 'The baby! the baby!' "

Then White placed Mary Lee in the back of his police car and drove to Temple Hospital at top speed with his siren blaring.

At 1:30 p.m. doctors at Temple Hospital declared the seventh Noe baby dead on arrival, noting that she appeared well-fed and cared for with no bruises to the body. She had also been carefully dressed in a white undershirt, diaper, plastic pants and a white knit shirt with high shoes and socks.

Soon afterwards Marie called Dr. Gangemi with the simple announcement: "Mary Lee is dead." Astonished by her coolness in the circumstances, Dr. Gangemi later expressed surprise at how any mother could deliver such horrible news in such an "emotionless and flat tone." He noted that it was totally in contrast with the excited concern she had shown on the numerous occasions she had previously called him about the baby.

Ninety minutes after Mary Lee's death, police drove Arthur and Marie Noe to the 25th District station for an interrogation. During the seventy-minute interview detectives James Cliggett and Joseph Fox questioned her about Mary Lee and the deaths of her other six children. They were startled by her reply.

"They all seemed to go very fast," she said. "Almost the same way as Mary did."

A few minutes later she casually told the detectives that she was already three months pregnant. Although Cliggett and Fox were satisfied with her explanation of Mary Lee's death, they still insisted on driving Marie and Arthur home for a closer look at their living conditions.

In their subsequent report the detectives noted that 3447 N. American Street was reasonably clean and well-heated. They inspected the crib in the front second-floor bedroom, where Mary Lee had died, and found it clean with a sheet on it. Nearby on a dresser they saw a half-finished bottle of red medicine that Dr. Gangemi had recently prescribed.

But they never bothered to interview Arthur's parents as they appeared too senile to be able to help.

On January 8, 1963, Arthur and Marie Noe buried their seventh baby and made the front pages of both the *Philadelphia Daily News* and the *Evening Bulletin*. Where the Noes' plight had once been confined to the streets of Kensington, now the whole of Philadelphia knew about their dead babies.

"Each time it happens, you die a little bit more and you get a little bit older," Arthur had told an *Evening Bulletin* reporter the previous night. "This funeral is the worst of all."

Prior to the funeral, the grieving family attended a memorial service at the Wildey Funeral Home on Front and Westmoreland Streets. Then Marie and Arthur buried their seventh infant at New Cathedral Cemetery, just around the corner from their home.

"It's God's will, I guess," said the bereaved father, wiping a tear from his eye. "This time we thought we had it licked. [Mary Lee] lived longer than any of the others—six months and fifteen days. We thought we were past the crucial part. We thought she was going to live."

Soon after the story appeared, Arthur Noe wrote a letter to the editor of the Philadelphia *Daily News*, thanking readers for their outpouring of sympathy for his family.

"Recently you printed a story of the death of our small daughter Mary," he wrote. "We wish to thank the *Daily News* and its wonderful readers from whom we have received cards and letters of sympathy and hope. Also all those that have given us their blessings.

"Never have my wife and I found such comfort and peace of mind simply from facing the realization that there are still lots of wonderful people in this world of ours. To you and to them we give our heartfelt thanks. [Signed] Mr. and Mrs. A. Noe."

Soon after the funeral Arthur Noe filed a claim with the Sun Life Insurance Company for the $1,250 policy taken out on Mary Lee, listing both parents as joint beneficiaries. The Baltimore-based company—which had already paid out on Arthur Jr. and Constance—suspected something was amiss and, after making the $1,250 payment, began investigating the Noes.

A month after Mary Lee's death, insurance investigator Paul Patterson paid an unannounced visit to N. American Street. Elizabeth Noe answered the door and told him that her daughter-in-law was at work. He gave her his card and left.

Two hours later Marie telephoned the investigator, explaining that her mother-in-law had been mistaken in saying that she had been at work. She willingly answered his questions about Mary Lee, pointing out that the coroner had still not determined her cause of death.

Patterson then put in a call to Detective Buckenhorst of the Philadelphia District Attorney's Office, who told him that his office was also looking into the Noes. It finally looked as if the authorities were determined to solve the riddle of Marie Noe's seven dead babies once and for all.

SEVEN

A RED HERRING

If the Philadelphia medical examiner and the district attorney's office thought it would be a straightforward investigation, they were in for a shock. No one wanted to accuse a mother of murdering her child without hard and fast evidence and infant death was often impossible to prove.

Then in the midst of the Noe baby deaths the whole perception of infant mortality dramatically changed with the introduction of a new theory called Crib Death. Gathering social and political momentum, Sudden Infant Death Syndrome (SIDS), as it would be dubbed in 1969, would provide an alibi that would help Marie Noe, and others like her, escape justice for a generation.

Infanticide has existed throughout history, with many cultures turning a blind eye to the murder of babies by impoverished mothers who couldn't afford to feed them. China had a long-standing tradition of killing infant girls, as they were considered inferior to boys. In ancient Greece, babies were buried alive in temple columns as sacrifices to the gods. In Medieval England infants were actually imprisoned in the structure of bridges to please the gods who would, presumably, keep them from falling as was the case when the first stone London Bridge was erected in 1176—in fact the line "Take a key and lock her up," in the popular nursery rhyme "London

Bridge is Falling Down," referred to these unfortunate children. In the Middle Ages infanticide was so rampant that the church elevated it from a venial sin to a mortal one, to try and eradicate it.

"The killing of newborns has been practiced in [Ireland] for centuries," wrote Australian author Susan Chenery in her book *Talking Dirty*. "The bodies of newborn babies are still discovered in fields and rivers around the country, poor country girls still unable to face the shame of an illegitimate child. No matter that she may have been raped or been the victim of incest."

Often these unfortunate babies were deliberately suffocated, leaving no evidence of any foul play. Nobody ever questioned their deaths as they were not considered *real* people in any sense of the word.

It wasn't until the end of the eighteenth century that French doctors began doing autopsies on babies to try and determine cause of death. They noticed that babies who died mysteriously often had enlarged thymus glands, concluding that the flow of oxygen to the brain was cut off by the enlarged gland. This unproved and erroneous theory of sudden infant death persisted right into the twentieth century.

When the thymus theory was debunked in the 1940s there was nothing to take its place. And doctors began diagnosing many of the thousands of baby deaths that occurred annually in the United States as "unexplained" or "unknown."

Former Philadelphia pathologist Dr. Dimitri Contostavlos said: "Up to the 1950s if a baby was found dead in bed there was great suspicion that [the mother] was responsible. She had either lain on top of it or she'd deliberately killed it.

"But then the pendulum swung the other way. Accusing the mother was considered cruel and it became unpopular to even suspect any wrong-doing."

While Marie Noe's babies were dying, a multitude of crib death theories abounded, making it one of the biggest mysteries of modern medicine. Some doctors believed it was caused by an allergy to cow's milk, while others blamed a blood disorder. Medical journals regularly highlighted the debate, printing theories from experts, ranging from respiratory infection to choking on baby formula.

The morbid question captured the public's imagination and every new mother felt a personal stake in the cause of crib death being discovered as soon as possible.

By 1962 Dr. Molly Valdes-Dapena had quietly emerged as the world's leading authority on infant death. Four years earlier, frustrated by the lack of evidence she found doing hundreds of baby autopsies at the Philadelphia Medical Examiner's Office, she decided to quit.

But Dr. Spelman, who was fascinated by the mystery, persuaded her to stay. He pointed out that unexplained infant death was a vital new branch of medical research which she could make her own, as it was virtually being ignored by everyone else.

Over the next few years Molly Dapena brought a pioneering, maverick spirit to the subject as she debunked theory after theory. She also published a well-received book on the subject called "Normal Histology of the Infant."

On August 7, 1963, crib death became front-page news when President John F. Kennedy's third child Patrick was born prematurely with a respiratory problem in Boston Children's Hospital. Two days later he was dead, with doctors labeling the cause "crib death."

"He put up quite a fight," a weeping President Kennedy told *Life* magazine, less than four months before his assassination in Dallas.

That September, Dr. Molly Dapena flew to Seattle to attend the first-ever international conference of health professionals called to discuss crib death and determine a strategy to solve it. Ironically, as she stepped up to the podium to address the thirty-seven delegates on her chosen field of expertise, Dr. Dapena was pregnant with her eleventh child.

After her speech a fellow expert asked about her involvement with the Noe babies, which had become the most prolific known case of serial crib death in a single American family.

"I talked for about a minute about it," remembered Dr. Dapena in 1998. "I gave them the details about the family."

Dr. Dapena briefly summarized how Marie Noe had lost seven babies in fifteen years, all but one in unexplained circumstances, and how none of the autopsies on the other six Noe babies had revealed any conclusive evidence on cause of death. But incredibly there was no interest whatsoever in this from the delegates.

"The next person who spoke jumped to a different subject altogether," recalled Dapena. "It aroused not one iota of further conversation among all those pediatric pathologists at the time. Nobody said, 'It can't be!' because in those days we didn't know. Now we all know. If it happens once, that's acceptable. The second one is really only a surprise and you investigate. No medical examiner would call a third 'crib death.' It's murder!"

*   *   *

As Philadelphia police and insurance investigators probed Marie Noe and her husband Arthur, medical examiner Dr. Joseph Spelman turned Mary Lee's body over to his assistant, Dr. Halbert E. Fillinger, Jr., for autopsy. An outgoing, gregarious thirty-six-year-old forensic pathologist, Dr. Fillinger specialized in unusual and complex pathological cases. A curious combination of physician and policeman, he would spend the next thirty-five years trying to solve the riddle of the Noe baby deaths.

Serving in the United States Navy in World War II, Fillinger transferred to the Army at the end of the war. On discharge he studied at the University of Wisconsin, obtaining a Bachelor of Science degree. Then he moved to Germany and the University of Heidelberg, where he became a doctor of medicine in 1955.

On his return to America he decided to specialize in forensic pathology, training in Cleveland and Toledo, before joining the Philadelphia Medical Examiner's Office in 1960. He would remain there for twenty-eight years, working on some of the city's most notorious murder cases.

In his initial examination of Mary Lee Noe's body, Dr. Fillinger was not looking for signs of murder. He was far more concerned that the seventh Noe baby might hold the key to the crib death mystery.

But as he embarked on his two-month examination, he admitted to the *Philadelphia Daily News* that the coincidence of death striking seven babies in one family was "bizarre."

"Here was a lady who might have some genetic defect that explained why people have SIDS deaths," he recalled in 1998. "While everybody was suspicious that they might not be dying natural death, we were all hoping that she might be part of the key of unlocking our crib death problem. But unfortunately it was not to be."

Working closely with Molly Dapena, the OME's on-site consultant, Dr. Fillinger now sought a research grant to carefully monitor Marie Noe's eighth pregnancy for clues.

Dr. Fillinger kept an open mind, although he thought that if it did turn out to be murder, the husband was more likely to have done it. Years later he would describe Arthur Noe as a "little bandy rooster of a guy who was feisty [and] troublesome." He saw Marie as a "bovine, docile, tranquil lady, not strikingly intellectually gifted."

Halfway through his autopsy Dr. Fillinger met with Philadelphia homicide detectives to compare notes.

"They had nothing to go on," he remembers. "They don't usually do much unless it's ruled murder. The routine investigations didn't turn up anything really suspicious except just a number of babies that were dying. And that's not enough to arrest somebody."

In mid-January, Juvenile Division policewoman Theresa Martin was assigned to the investigation and accompanied Detective Joseph Fox to 3447 N. American Street to question the Noes.

"There were suspicions among myself and other detectives that the children had died under unusual circumstances," she recalled in 1998.

While Detective Fox was closely questioning Marie and Arthur Noe about the deaths of their babies, Martin looked on, astonished at their composure and apparent lack of emotion.

"We were all surprised," Martin remembered. "[Marie] showed very little emotion and neither did her husband. We all had our suspicions about the Noes, but we could never prove anything."

By mid-March, Fillinger and Dapena had managed to secure a grant from St. Christopher's Hospital to cover all of Marie Noe's medical expenses for her next child, in exchange for allowing it to be genetically studied and monitored. But the Noes rejected the offer on the advice of Dr. Gangemi, who told them he was just as qualified to supervise Marie's pregnancy as any publicity-seeking physicians. He warned them that the hospital would probably take away their new baby and raise it in laboratory conditions.

Today Dr. Fillinger believes that Dr. Gangemi, who had wanted to run the project and unsuccessfully applied to be lead investigator, had ulterior motives in persuading the Noes not to cooperate.

On March 16, a frustrated Dr. Fillinger announced that his exhaustive tests on Mary Lee's body had failed to reveal the cause of death. He would officially record it as "undetermined."

"We have been unable to pinpoint the cause," he told the Philadelphia *Evening Bulletin*. "All we can say is that it was a natural death."

He explained his close collaboration with doctors from St. Christopher's Hospital to try and solve the riddle of what was killing the Noe babies.

"We found no disease, no injury. Every test turned out negative," he stated.

On June 28th, 1963, Marie Noe went into premature labor and was rushed to St. Joseph's Hospital, just one day after her father-in-law Charles Noe died at their home. At thirty-eight weeks she gave birth to a five-and-a-half-pound baby girl, who was delivered by cesarean section. Theresa Noe lived just six hours and thirty-nine minutes and died in the hospital without her parents even seeing her.

"I guess we weren't meant to have babies," was Marie Noe's only comment when she heard of Theresa's death.

But when the medical examiner's office released Theresa's autopsy results it muddied the waters for all investigations into the Noes. For the cause of death was given as a blood disorder, congenital hemorrhagic; a condition not detected in·any of the strenuous medical tests on the other babies or the parents.

Dr. Halbert Fillinger says that Theresa's death totally "confounded" him.

With two out of the last three Noe babies dying of natural causes in the hospital, the investigators now scratched their heads as the case took a baffling new turn and continued to defy any known medical logic.

"There has to be a cause and we're still trying to find it," a frustrated Dr. Gangemi told the *Philadelphia Inquirer*, despite the suspicions he secretly harbored against the Noes. "If we could only find the answer we'd have a story that would benefit the profession and people who have been losing children."

In July, Marie and Arthur Noe were catapulted to national attention when they were the subject of a two-page special report in *Life* magazine. Using the pseudonyms Andrew and Martha Moore, *Life* writer Mary H. Cadwalader chronicled the Noes' story in harrowing detail.

But as she interviewed Arthur and Marie in their front

room at N. American Street, Cadwalader too was amazed by the lack of emotion they displayed in recounting the tragic deaths of their babies.

"I thought that was odd," she would remember thirty-five years later. "I guess I expected a much more emotional interview. But they were rather cool and cold about it. They had lost all these children and I wondered if there was anything darker going on. But of course the police hadn't found anything to charge them with."

Directly after interviewing the Noes, Cadwalader drove into Philadelphia to meet with Dr. Molly Dapena, then in the midst of Mary Lee's autopsy, seeking a SIDS overview for her story.

"The mothers are haunted," Dr. Dapena told her, adding that the Noes were a unique SIDS case. "They ask, 'What did I do wrong?' They can't forgive themselves. I don't know what to tell them, except that we don't know. We simply don't know."

After the official interview was over, Dr. Dapena, curious about Marie Noe, whom she had never met in person, asked Cadwallader for her impressions about her.

"She said that it was one of the strangest experiences that she had ever had," recalled Dr. Dapena in 1998. "Because this woman sat on her rocking chair on her front porch and talked about all these deaths without any change of expression whatsoever in her face. Not a tear. Nothing. Nothing. She was perfectly placid about the whole thing. I'll always remember that writer telling me that."

When the story came out in July, Cadwalader put her own personal feelings to one side to cast Marie Noe as a martyr, swiftly elevating her to the status of America's most famous bereaved mother.

"Worn almost to gauntness, and stung by sharp-eyed stares from her neighbors," wrote Cadwalader, "[Marie Noe] spent several days in the hospital this spring in an effort to build up her health and spirit and restore some sense of equilibrium. Her eyes are two enormous dark smudges in a face as gray as ashes.

"She seldom visits the children's graves. Courage, in her lexicon, counts more than tears. She stays close to home with her dog and her two cats. Life and its chores go on in the humble frame house, shadowed by a frail, poignant hope.

"For [Marie] had not wanted [Mary Lee] to be an only child. Her eighth baby will be born this month."

Soon after the *Life* story appeared, Arthur Noe, furious at not being financially compensated for the interview, wanted to sue the magazine for invasion of privacy. But his attorney and neighbor Daniel Maxymuik strongly advised him to drop the matter immediately.

On August 3, 1963, the recently widowed Elizabeth Noe was taken ill and admitted to Philadelphia General Hospital with heart disease. Three days later her Philadelphia National Bank savings account was mysteriously closed and all moneys withdrawn. As Elizabeth was illiterate and used an "X" as a signature it would prove impossible to discover who had closed the account while she was confined to a hospital bed.

After an eleven-day stay she was discharged and Arthur took her home. But only days later he placed her in the Blair Nursing and Convalescent Home on Old York Avenue in Philadelphia, where she was diagnosed with malnutrition.

The nursing home had been arranged by a Philadelphia General Hospital social worker who had negotiated a special rate for her. Her son had agreed to pay $60 a month in addition to her own $155 allowance from the Department of Public Assistance. But once she was in the home he refused to pay a cent.

Blair assistant administrator Dorothy Bolger would later tell OME investigator Joe McGillen how both Arthur and Marie appeared to hate the sickly old woman.

"[They had a] beastly disregard for his mother," Bolger remembered, adding that she felt that either one of them would be fully capable of harming others. Bolger told McGillen that the Noes showed absolutely no interest in Elizabeth once they had left her there. And they only came to visit when specifically asked to do so by the staff.

They also failed to provide the home with any clothes for Elizabeth and only did so grudgingly after a flood of phone calls from administrators.

During Elizabeth Noe's two-month stay, Mrs. Bolger repeatedly asked Arthur to pay the $60 a month toward his mother's keep. Each time she called him in to discuss the matter he would fly into a rage, becoming "hostile and belligerent."

Although by this time the elderly Noe matriarch was senile, she would have moments of lucidity and accuse her daughter-in-law of stealing her bankbooks. She told nurses that she had an account at a bank on Frankford Avenue but was unable to remember its name.

Convinced she was telling the truth, Mrs. Bolger started an investigation into the missing money. But in October, while a caseworker was trying to locate the bank, Arthur Noe got wind of what was happening and suddenly transferred his mother to the Riverview Home for the Aged on State Road in Philadelphia.

Once again Arthur Noe agreed to pay the old people's home something toward his mother's keep, but never did. Elizabeth Noe was eventually designated a city charity case after her son ran up arrears of $500, which was later written off by the city social services as uncollectable.

Elizabeth Noe's physical and mental condition continued to deteriorate and after eight months at Riverview she was admitted to Philadelphia General Hospital, where she died of heart disease on June 8th.

Within days of her death, Arthur and Marie cashed in the life insurance policy they had taken out on her.

EIGHT

CATHY NOE

While her mother-in-law lay dying in an old people's home in early 1964, Marie Noe became pregnant again. Dr. Gangemi confirmed the news but was secretly concerned about the baby's chances of survival. Although he considered his patient an unstable schizophrenic, possibly psychotic, all he could do was sit back and let fate take its course.

In November, when Marie was eight months pregnant, Dr. Gangemi put her under hypnosis, installing a series of post-hypnotic suggestions to improve her maternal skills. During the session he attempted to increase her self-confidence, so she'd remain calm if her new baby became cranky or cried.

"I suggested to her that she would keep her composure and remain tranquil when caring for the child," he would later tell OME investigators.

At one point during the session the doctor considered asking Marie if she had killed her children. But he decided against it, knowing that any confession made under hypnosis could not be used in court.

He also taught her self-hypnosis to help her calm down at home. To this day Marie routinely hypnotizes herself for ten to twenty minutes every morning after breakfast, awakening from her trance when her husband comes downstairs.

When the Noes' ninth baby, Catherine Ellen, was born by c-section at St. Joseph's Hospital on December 3, 1964, Dr. Gangemi breathed a sigh of relief as Marie agreed for her new baby to remain in the hospital indefinitely. Concerned that the cherubic-looking, seven-pound seven-ounce baby girl was in danger, Dr. Gangemi deliberately stalled for time, ordering her to be kept under strict observation and given an exhaustive range of tests. Once Catherine left the hospital and went home, Dr. Gangemi knew she would be on her own and he would not be able to help her.

Months later he would confide that he prayed that "the baby's fingernails grow long enough so she would have a chance to defend herself."

Cathy spent the first three months of her life at St. Joseph's, where her cheerful disposition endeared her to all the nurses on the pediatric ward. Many of the staff were nuns from the Sisters of St. Felix, a convent based in Lodi, New Jersey. The head nurse was a nun in her early twenties named Sister Victorine, who would become especially close to Cathy and try to protect her.

Later Sister Victorine would remember Cathy as being an exceptionally happy baby who never had any trouble during her prolonged hospital stays. The only problems occurred when her parents came to visit.

The chubby little baby ate well and made good progress in her first few weeks of life. She was carefully monitored for any symptoms of illness or congenital defects, in light of her parents' past history.

While in the hospital, Cathy had regular visits from the Noes. Each time they came Sister Victorine carefully observed how they interacted with their new daughter. "Mr. Noe always was much more affectionate toward the child than Mrs. Noe, [who] seemed to prefer to remain detached and aloof and dispassionate in her feelings," Sister Victorine would later tell investigators.

She also noticed a distinct change in Marie's behavior whenever other people were present. She would become far more affectionate toward Cathy, as if she felt it was expected. "At these times she would utter inane little offerings that would have no bearing on the moment," said the Sister. "[We] always felt these unrelated remarks were born most probably out of a peculiar need by Mrs. Noe to say something, anything."

Another pediatric supervisor, Sister Mary Gemma, would later back up Sister Victorine's assessment, adding that there were times when Marie "acted like two distinctly different persons."

By the beginning of March, Dr. Gangemi reluctantly discharged Cathy from St. Joseph's as there was no medical reason to keep her any longer. Back at home the Noes' friends and family held their breath to see if Cathy would share the sad fate of her brothers and sisters.

"Cathy was a beautiful baby," said her Aunt Anne. "She looked just like her mother. Only Marie had big blue eyes and the baby had brown ones."

Two weeks after Cathy left the hospital the Sun Life Insurance Company rejected Arthur Noe's application for a $1,000 insurance policy on her life. They deemed it a bad risk, after having to pay out on the other Noe babies.

In Kensington that summer it became a familiar sight to see Marie Noe proudly pushing her daughter around the neighborhood in a new red carriage. But many of her neighbors felt she was acting stranger than ever, as she now refused to acknowledge them on the street.

"Sometimes [Marie] will say 'hello' to you and other times she doesn't even seem to notice you," her long-time neighbor Rosella Heilemann recalled.

Another neighbor, Carrie McDonald, thought it "odd" that Marie would often walk past old friends on the street whom she had known for years, as if she'd never seen them before.

"[I've] seen her walking the various babies in the carriage from time to time," she would tell investigators the following year. "They all appeared to be healthy and normal children and well cared for. They were always clean and neatly dressed."

When Cathy turned eight months old in August, she became the longest surviving Noe baby. To celebrate, Arthur and Marie took their pudgy, rosy-cheeked daughter to New York to visit the World's Fair and then to the beach. During the trip Arthur took lots of photographs of his daughter and began a photo album to record her development.

Every evening Marie would spend hours carefully placing each picture of the beautiful infant in the album with infinite care. Then she would write a caption, giving Cathy's exact age and when and where it had been taken. It was like she was keeping a memento of her little daughter for posterity, in case she didn't survive.

But everything changed after the Noes returned from their New York vacation. On August 31, a distressed Marie telephoned Dr. Gangemi saying that she had just discovered Cathy in her crib, choking on a plastic dry cleaning bag which had become wrapped around her head. Marie explained that the infant, who could barely crawl, had somehow stood up and pulled the bag off one of Arthur Noe's suits, which had been hanging in a nearby closet.

Dr. Gangemi was "horrified" and did not believe Marie's explanation. His patience had finally run out and he could no longer pretend that nothing was wrong. "Now, how could an eight-month-old baby get hold of a large sheet of plastic off a suit hanging in the closet?" he finally snapped.

Completely unfazed by the doctor's outburst, Marie never missed a beat as she coolly replied that she had no idea how it could have happened, and how "fortunate" it was that she'd found her in time.

The doctor then ordered her to take Cathy to St. Joseph's Hospital, where she'd be safe. Later, when questioned about the incident, Arthur would contradict his wife by insisting that his suit wasn't in a closet at all. It was, he said, hanging on a bar he'd set up between two side walls to create extra closet space. But the mystery remained as to how a tiny toddler could possibly have reached the potentially lethal plastic bag hanging so high above her head in a closet.

When Cathy was admitted to the pediatric ward she was in a state of terror. The nurses were shocked that the little baby, previously so happy, now continually cried as if she had colic. Although a physical examination found nothing wrong with Cathy, it took the nuns forty-eight hours to calm her down into the smiling little angel they remembered.

During Cathy's prolonged stays in St. Joseph's Hospital, Marie would constantly complain about her baby being off her food and refusing to eat. So, in line with hospital regulations, Sister Victorine encouraged Marie to feed her baby and develop a maternal bond. But Cathy always seemed terrified of her mother, and would not eat whenever she visited. Yet as soon as Marie left, the nurses would feed her without any trouble. Cathy would be all smiles as she eagerly cleared her plate.

On one occasion Sister Victorine deliberately left Cathy alone with her mother in the kitchen adjoining the pediatric ward, to see what would happen. There she observed Marie attempt to force food down Cathy's throat after the baby refused to eat.

When this failed, Sister Victorine was horrified to hear Marie angrily hiss, "You better take this or I'll kill you!" When she rushed into the kitchen to protect Cathy, Marie began making baby talk and pretended that nothing had happened.

While Cathy was in the hospital, Arthur Noe tried once again to insure his daughter's life. This time he was successful, using a political contact he had made while working as a Democratic committeeman, who arranged a $1,500 policy through a local agent in Philadelphia.

After Cathy's five-week stay in the hospital, many of the nuns had grown emotionally attached to the pretty little girl, showering her with the love and attention she appeared to be deprived of at home. And when she was discharged on October 6, the nurses were upset and frightened for her safety. Some even wondered if they would ever see her alive again.

"We were afraid of sending her home," said Sister Mary Gemma in 1998, "because of the past deaths in the family."

Soon after discharge, Marie Noe began calling Dr. Gangemi incessantly about anything that she felt was wrong with Cathy. Later he would view this as the beginning of a disturbing new pattern of incidents when Marie claimed to find her child "turning blue" or "having a seizure."

In one instance Marie claimed she was carrying her daughter to Dr. Gangemi's office when she suddenly went limp. She rushed Cathy home and called the rescue squad, who revived her with oxygen and took her to Episcopal Hospital. When Marie told Dr. Gangemi, he immediately arranged to have Cathy re-admitted to St. Joseph's.

The curly-haired blonde child spent her first birthday—a milestone no other Noe baby would ever attain— in the hospital on December 3, 1965. To celebrate, the nuns held a birthday party on the ward, which was attended by her parents. Arthur proudly took photos of his little daughter in her new red party dress, as she happily posed and clapped her hands in delight. On a bed nearby Marie sat alone, looking nervous and uncomfortable.

The following day Marie Noe was a changed woman. She surprised the nurses by bursting into the ward to show off her favorite picture from Cathy's birthday party.

"Usually she was quite introverted and showed no outward affection for her baby," remembered Sister Mary Gemma. "[She came in and] showed the nuns and nurses a colored photograph of Cathy which they all thought was quite nice."

The next morning Marie returned armed with a batch of prints she'd had made from the photograph. She then proceeded to make the rounds, proudly handing them out to doctors, nurses and administrative staff all over the hospital, as if she were some kind of a celebrity.

Recalled Sister Mary Gemma: "The nuns and nurses

in the maternity ward, the operating room and in the pediatrics ward all got copies of the picture without ever requesting them."

Once again, after a three-week hospital stay, the nuns sadly kissed Cathy good-bye as her parents took her home. But they wouldn't have to wait long to see her again.

On Christmas Eve—just eight days after Cathy's discharge—Marie called the rescue squad, saying that her daughter had "blacked out" and was having "a spell." And when the poor little girl was brought back to St. Joseph's she was petrified and inconsolable.

"She was a beautiful kid," said Sister Mary Gemma. "But she was frightened and stand-offish. She wouldn't come to you."

Eventually the nuns managed to calm Cathy down and stop her crying. From then on Sister Mary Gemma and the pediatric nurses watched Marie Noe like hawks whenever she visited to ensure no harm would come to Cathy.

"[Mrs. Noe] had a flat-affect," Sister Mary Gemma would later tell police. "She showed little or no emotion. On each [visit] she was watched closely by myself and the staff, because [we] were concerned for Catherine's welfare due to the family history."

In the total six months she spent in the hospital Cathy never had a respiratory problem or any other ailment. And Dr. Gangemi and the nurses could find no *natural* reason for the constant "spells" and "black-outs" she suffered at home.

"That's why we were all suspicious," said Sister Mary Gemma. "Because nothing ever happened in the hospital. She did great maturing in the hospital. She was normal in every way: eating, walking and other activities of living. She responded in a positive way to the nurturing she received [from] the pediatric staff."

Cathy spent her second Christmas in the hospital being fussed over by the nuns. During the festive season Arthur and Marie pretended that all was well with their daughter. Whenever neighbors or shopkeepers inquired about Cathy's health, they would reply that she was fine.

On January 19, 1966, Arthur Noe arrived at St. Joseph's and insisted on taking Cathy home. Fearing for the toddler's safety, Dr. Gangemi was against it but was legally powerless to prevent him discharging his daughter. But he did manage to persuade Arthur to buy a tank of Lif-O-Gen, an oxygen delivery system, in case Cathy suffered another "spell."

Once home, Arthur Noe took other precautions to protect his daughter. He erected a screen door on her bedroom, so they could keep a close watch on her, and placed a walkie-talkie by her crib, carefully taping the "talk" button down so she could be monitored around the clock.

When Cathy came home the Noes celebrated a belated family Christmas. Under a Christmas tree in the front room, Arthur and Marie unwrapped the gifts they had bought their daughter, including a baby doll set complete with stroller, a tricycle, a miniature telephone system and a spelling game.

A few days later Marie Noe dressed Cathy in her new red-and-white party frock and brought her to Dr. Gangemi's office with Arthur.

"They just came to show off the little girl," remembers Dr. Gangemi's medical assistant, Maria Datillio. "She was a pretty little girl. The father just looked at her and beamed. The mother just sat smiling at the doctor. All I could say to myself [was], 'Thank God this one is alive!' "

The following Saturday night Arthur left his wife at home to look after Cathy while he went off to the taproom to drink beer with his friends. While he was out Marie claimed to have walked into the bedroom and discovered the little girl having "a slight seizure." She revived her with oxygen and called Dr. Gangemi, who made a house call. When he couldn't find anything wrong with the child, he prescribed the children's version of the anti-seizure medicine Dilantin.

Two weeks later on Valentine's Day, Marie Noe again telephoned Dr. Gangemi in a panic. This time she reported finding Cathy turning blue in her playpen, after she'd walked in with her laundry. Realizing Cathy was in trouble, Marie claimed to have grabbed the Lif-O-Gen tank and attempted to give her oxygen. But her jaws seized up and her "tongue was between her teeth."

When Dr. Gangemi arrived he could find nothing wrong with the fourteen-month-old child. Later he would tell investigators that he always had "real doubts" about Marie Noe's tall stories.

The following Sunday, Arthur drove his wife and daughter to Norristown, Pennsylvania, to attend a social day organized by the Fraternal Order of Orioles, of which he was a long-time member. He particularly wanted his fellow Orioles to see his infant daughter, who was wearing a new dress he'd bought especially for the occasion. She was the center of attention, as everybody fussed over her and congratulated Arthur and Marie on having such a wonderful little girl.

Three days later on Thursday, February 24, the Noes

went to bed early after watching television with Cathy. The next morning Marie got up and did her self-hypnosis exercises and then cooked breakfast for her husband.

After he left for work she bathed and dressed Cathy, taking her to a nearby grocery store to buy food. On their return, Marie thought the toddler looked tired, so she put her in her playpen to nap. Then she went into the kitchen to do the laundry.

Later she would claim that she heard Cathy fall down at about 11:00 a.m. and rushed into the living room to find her unconscious and turning blue. It was a bizarre carbon copy of what had happened on St. Valentine's Day. But this time Cathy was dead.

During her dramatic 1998 confession, when asked if she had killed Cathy, Marie replied cryptically: "I can't remember if I did anything to her or not."

Neighbor Marie Maxymuik, who lived two doors away from the Noes, was home with her two young children when Marie hysterically telephoned for help.

"I ran to the Noes' home and Marie was home alone with Catherine," said Mrs. Maxymuik, whose attorney husband Daniel represented Arthur Noe. "I can remember that Catherine wasn't awake, she was unconscious. I don't remember her being blue, so that I felt she might have been alive."

Mrs. Maxymuik bundled her young son Nicholas, who was one of Cathy's playmates, into the back of her car and drove off to Episcopal Hospital with Marie holding her daughter in the front seat. It took twenty minutes to reach the hospital, due to the heavy morning traffic, and throughout the journey Mrs. Maxymuik kept reassuring Marie that everything would be all right.

At 11:05 a.m. Marie brought Cathy—wearing pink overalls and a white shirt—into the emergency room and told doctors that the baby was not breathing. A Dr. Jacobs, who was on duty, examined Cathy and found no vital signs so he immediately administered adrenaline straight into her heart. At 11:20 a.m. Dr. Jacobs pronounced Cathy Noe dead, noting no obvious physical injuries.

A few minutes later Marie Noe telephoned Dr. Gangemi with the grim news. Maria Datillio took the call, immediately transferring it to the doctor, who became visibly angry on hearing Marie's explanation.

As he slowly put down the phone he looked as pale as a sheet as he told his assistant: "Get me the police—the Noe baby died."

When Datillio asked him if she could do anything, he walked straight back into his office. "No, I'll take care of this myself," he said sternly, slamming the door behind him.

A few minutes later Datillio went into his office and Dr. Gangemi said sadly: "There was nothing wrong with that baby."

"We never discussed it again," Datillio would tell detectives in 1998. "He just said that one thing."

NINE

AN ADOPTION APPLICATION

As preparations were made to transfer Cathy Noe's body to the city morgue, the medical examiner's office launched a full-scale investigation. Within two hours of her death, Philadelphia Medical Examiner Joseph Spelman had assigned his two best investigators to the case.

Joseph McGillen was no stranger to Marie and Arthur Noe. A casually dressed, genial man, whose easy-going manner belied the sharp, calculating brain of a detective, McGillen had first interviewed the Noes in early 1963 after Mary Lee's death. Over the next thirty-five years the highly methodical medical detective would constantly ponder the most frustrating case of his career.

Also assigned to the case was Remington Bristow, a hard-nosed sleuth with a soft center who wore the sharply defined features of a Dick Tracy cartoon like a badge of honor. A few years earlier his young son had died, leaving him utterly distraught. Now whenever called upon to probe an infant's death, Bristow became personally involved, way beyond the call of duty.

By February 1966, he was already nine years into a personal crusade to solve Philadelphia's infamous "Boy in the Box Case." He had been summoned to the crime scene after the naked body of a four-year-old boy was discovered in a cardboard packing box in the woods outside the city. With few clues to go on, Rem Bristow would devote the rest of his life to identifying the boy, so he could have a proper burial, and bringing the murderer to justice.

For many years fresh flowers would regularly be placed on the grave of the "Boy in the Box" by a mysterious well-wisher. Eventually the grave's secret caretaker was unmasked as the rugged OME investigator, still in mourning for his own dead son. Now nine years later Rem Bristow found himself in the center of a series of infant deaths that defied medical explanation. It moved him to his very soul.

At 1:30 p.m. on the day of Cathy's death, McGillen and Bristow arrived at Episcopal Hospital. There they were met by Philadelphia Police Detective Sakoff who was already interviewing Arthur and Marie Noe.

The two investigators arranged to meet the Noes a little later at their home and proceeded to the accident ward where Cathy's body was lying on a bed. She was still wearing a jumper, shirt, undershirt, shoes, socks, diaper and wet rubber pants.

Peering through his steel-rimmed spectacles, McGillen did a cursory external examination but could find no signs of injury. He noted the body was bluish and still warm, and rigor mortis had not yet set in. There was also a white liquid coming from the nose and mouth. After making some notes he arranged for the body to be transported to the medical examiner's office for autopsy.

At 2:00 p.m. McGillen and Bristow drew up to 3447 N. American Street where the Noes were already waiting for them. A few minutes later their lawyer, Daniel Maxymuik, whose wife had earlier rushed Marie to the hospital, arrived. He told the investigators he had come to ensure that the Noes "get a fair shake, because the last time this happened they were put through hell by the police."

McGillen and Bristow then toured the two-storey house, making careful notes as they searched for clues. McGillen's subsequent report described the Noes' home as modestly furnished and in need of a coat of paint. But he noted that, although the house was in a poor state of repair, it boasted a gleaming new refrigerator, washer and dryer and portable TV. McGillen secretly wondered if the life insurance policies he knew Arthur Noe had taken out on the babies had financed these expensive appliances.

They then went to the downstairs living room where Cathy had died. It was plainly furnished with an old davenport and some faded armchairs. At the far end of the room they saw Cathy's playpen, which still had her favorite doll and other Christmas toys lying on it.

While Rem Bristow questioned Marie Noe in the kitchen, Joe McGillen deliberately took Arthur upstairs to the bedroom, so he couldn't influence his wife's answers. The seasoned investigator began quizzing him about Cathy but soon touched a raw nerve when he mentioned the *Life* article.

Wrote McGillen: "I asked him to what extent the family had been compensated by *Life* and he became indignant. 'Are you kidding? We never got a cent out of that.' "

Cunningly, McGillen sympathized with Arthur, who started to relax and become talkative. He spoke about his wife, saying she was far more religious than he was and had encouraged his return to the church. Although he admitted neither of them were very religious and rarely went to confession.

He also confided that he used to drink heavily but had recently cut down to please Marie. Now that Arthur Noe's defenses were down, McGillen subtly steered the conversation around to his children's untimely deaths and his wife's possible involvement.

"I asked him if he was at all curious about the fact that whenever something had happened to any of the children, including [Cathy] on several occasions, he was never at home," wrote McGillen.

"He admitted that it must naturally look suspicious to us but he insists that he has never entertained the slightest doubts about his wife in this respect."

Moving on, McGillen questioned Noe about his family finances and noticed that he began fidgeting and looking very uncomfortable. He told McGillen that he earned $212.34 (worth about $1080 today) every two weeks before taxes but refused to divulge how much he brought home, saying his wife took care of all finances.

Noe claimed to be in such dire financial straits that he was even behind with his milk bill. He told McGillen he owed more than $5,000 to various creditors and had used that month's $50 rent money to pay off his electricity and gas bills so they wouldn't be cut off.

The day after Cathy's death Marie and Arthur Noe went out shopping to buy new funeral outfits from Graff's Clothes on Kensington Avenue. Marie bought a smart black dress while her husband bought a new suit complete with an all-weather topcoat.

That evening they arrived home to find local newspaper reporters and photographers camped out on their front step. The bereaved parents immediately invited reporters from the *Philadelphia Inquirer* and *Daily News* into their front room for an impromptu interview. Prominently displayed on a table next to their sofa was an assortment of framed photographs of Cathy.

"I just don't know what we're going to do," Marie told the reporters in a soft, wavering voice. "We can't have any more children. It's too late."

Lighting up another cigarette, Arthur Noe asked the reporters to be sure and mention a Mass of the Angels he'd arranged in Cathy's memory at St. Hugh's Church.

Then Marie Noe calmly announced that they were now considering adoption, as at thirty-seven she was too old to have children. They said they planned to discuss it with their pastor at the earliest opportunity.

"They may not let us have one," Marie conceded, "on account of so many deaths."

Then, looking over at a photograph of her beautiful golden-curled daughter in her best blue party dress, Marie said: "We really thought we were going to make it this time. She looked just as healthy as anyone. A beautiful child."

And Marie told the reporters that since all the publicity about the deaths of their babies, they had been inundated with hate mail, blaming them for what had happened.

"One terrible thing about the deaths of our children has been the way people have acted," she declared, as her husband put his arm around her. "People have written to us and said that we shouldn't have had children. They were atheists and sick people. But there were kind letters too, and one woman who had two miscarriages said that our example had given her more faith."

When Dr. Gangemi read the highly sympathetic newspaper stories he shuddered in horror. Although the Noes would always claim they hated publicity, the doctor believed they relished their new-found celebrity status in Philadelphia and actively encouraged interviews.

"She loves attention," he would later tell investigators. "And when *Life* magazine did that article on her she was the center of attention and seemed to love every minute of it."

When Cathy's autopsy results were released they cast no new light on the mysterious cycle of Noe baby deaths. Assistant medical examiner Dr. Joseph E. Campbell, who performed the autopsy, could find no definite cause of death, ruling it "undetermined."

Although a spokesman for the medical examiner's office told reporters the official line that it had been a "typical crib death," Dr. Joseph Spelman was highly suspicious and quietly ordered a further round of additional tests.

After the autopsy was completed, Cathy's body was moved to the Wildey Funeral Home on Front and Westmoreland Streets, where the Noes had organized a public viewing. Among those who attended were Sisters Victorine and Mary Gemma, who were devastated by having their worst fears confirmed when their beloved Cathy died.

Holding back tears, the sisters walked into the funeral home and saw the little girl's body lying in a plain wooden casket. They shuddered, realizing that she was wearing the exact same outfit they had dressed her up in when Arthur Noe had collected her from St. Joseph's

Hospital. It was the last time they had ever seen her alive.

During the viewing the nuns noticed two small bouquets lying by the casket. One of them was from one of Cathy's aunts and read "Too Soon." The other, they presumed from the parents but unsigned, bore the message, "Our Baby."

On their way out the nuns asked the funeral director if they could have the bouquets after the funeral to place in their chapel as a reminder of Cathy. The following day Arthur and Marie Noe arrived at the hospital wearing black to personally place the flowers in the chapel. Then they went to the pediatric ward to thank Sister Victorine and her staff.

"Mr. Noe thanked [us] for everything [we] had done for the baby," said Sister Victorine, who has since left the order to become a missionary in South America. "He was choked up at the time. Mrs. Noe also seemed to be [upset] but she never uttered a single word to anyone."

The day after Cathy Noe was laid to rest next to her sisters Mary Lee and Constance at the New Cathedral Cemetery, her parents met with their parish priest to discuss adopting a baby. The father agreed that it seemed like a good idea and arranged an appointment for them the following day at the Philadelphia Catholic Archdiocese to fill out the necessary application forms.

By the time the Noes left St. Hugh's Church it was starting to get dark. As they walked down Tioga to N. American, the drab, row-house street was coming alive with the happy cries of children, returning home from school.

But as Arthur and Marie sadly shuffled past the railroad track to their house they felt a new optimism. Perhaps Arthur would get another chance at being a father and having his own family. He told his wife that he couldn't wait for them to be a *real* family again. Somehow she seemed less than enthusiastic about the idea.

Soon after they arrived home the doorbell rang and Arthur answered it. Standing at the door was Russ Green, a reporter from United Press International, and his photographer. The two had been assigned to do a human-interest story on the Noes and how they were coping with the loss of their ninth baby.

As Green had not called beforehand he was unsure how the bereaved couple would react to being interviewed at such a sad time in their lives.

After they announced themselves, Arthur Noe called out "It's some reporters!" to Marie, who was just finishing a telephone call in the dining room. She immediately came to the front door, saying: "No more publicity, please!" Then she saw the photographer and said she certainly didn't want pictures.

But then a strange thing happened. Green would later remember that, despite their initial opposition, his journalistic instincts told him that the Noes actually wanted to be interviewed. Almost immediately Arthur and Marie ushered them through the front door and sat them down in the dining room for a chat.

Green began talking generally, planning to take his time and subtly steer the conversation around to their dead children.

"[I] soon became aware that they were actually anxious to discuss them," recalled Green, who took notes for his story. Before long the Noes seemed to forget they were being interviewed by a reporter, openly discussing Cathy's death and their hopes to adopt a new baby.

"We had her so long," mused Marie Noe. "I kept seeing her such a nice young lady."

Asked how she was coping with the loss, Marie replied stoically: "I am just putting my thoughts together, just saying a few prayers. The house is so empty. All we want to do now is fill the void. It is our only hope now to fill the emptiness with an unwanted child of someone."

For most of the interview they seemed calm and collected but at one point Marie became uncharacteristically upset when Green asked if she intended to have any more natural children. Her pallid face flushed florid pink with emotion as she told Green that she couldn't bear going through another pregnancy without knowing what to expect after she gave birth.

"It's a hell," she suddenly cried, looking close to tears. "To look at them, to love them, to see them go like that! If we had another child, just the fear, not knowing from one day to the next."

And at another point in the interview, while discussing Cathy's death, Marie suddenly became extremely defensive.

"We wouldn't hurt her for the world," she blurted out to the reporter's astonishment. "I'd trade places with her but He wanted her instead of me!"

Later when Green wrote up the piece, syndicated to hundreds of newspapers all over America a week later, he deliberately omitted the telling words, "He wanted her instead of me!"

In the story, entitled "Philadelphia Couple Who Lost Nine Infants Seek to Adopt Baby," Green painted a poignant portrait of a heroic couple, bravely coming to terms with a tragedy of almost biblical proportions.

"It is a two-storey row house, like the dozens of other neat little row houses stretching up and down the streets. But it is marked by tragedy, starkly unanswerable tragedy, baffling and mysterious.

"The tragedy is death. Not death alone. That can be understandable. This is the chilling death of nine infants, none more than fourteen months old.

"They were the children of Arthur and Marie Noe, best described as just neighbors' neighbors. Roman Catholic parents who have lost their nine children by sudden, swift-striking illness since April of 1949."

Marie Noe was also cast in the role of a saintly neighborhood benefactor, telling the UPI reporter how she and Arthur had personally helped a mother of five get through a crisis by helping her husband find a job.

"Honestly, I never saw a more sorrowful case," Arthur Noe told Green. "I figured helping them did something good to me inside."

Observed Green: "That, from a father whose nine babies died."

The next morning Arthur and Marie drove into Philadelphia to the Catholic Children's Bureau to officially file for adoption. They were interviewed by the supervising nun, Sister Michael Marie, who helped them fill in the preliminary application forms to begin the lengthy adoption process.

The Noes listened carefully as the nun explained standard adoption procedure, pointing out that even if they were accepted, it could take nine months to a year before they would get a baby. In the meantime they would have to prepare a complete family history and allow a representative from the bureau to inspect their home.

If they passed these hurdles they would then have to attend a month-long series of group meetings along with other parents seeking to adopt. It was during this part of the process, Sister Michael warned, that a lot of couples dropped out. The Noes told the nun that they were so desperate to adopt a child, they would gladly go through all the screening processes if it would mean having a family again.

The following week Joe McGillen was horrified to read the UPI story announcing the Noes' intention to adopt a baby. He immediately telephoned Sister Michael Marie and confided his grave suspicions about the family. He asked whether the Catholic Children's Bureau routinely subjected parents to a psychiatric evaluation. She replied that although it wasn't standard practice, the bureau could order psychiatric testing if deemed necessary. Sister Michael Marie agreed to update McGillen on how the Noes' adoption application progressed in the ensuing months.

Six weeks later on April 20, Marie and Arthur Noe sat in on a group meeting of prospective parents at the Catholic Children's Bureau. The session was chaired by Sister Michael Marie, who noted how ill-kempt and untidy Mrs. Noe looked, although her husband was well dressed in his best suit. During the session the Noes frankly exchanged views on the adoption process with several other couples and discussed their reasons for seeking a child.

At the end of the session Sister Michael Marie casually asked Arthur Noe what he thought about the meeting. Incredibly, he told the nun how surprised he was that no one had asked "whether one was allowed to insure an adopted child."

Sister Michael Marie was staggered by the highly inappropriate question. She would later tell Joe McGillen that it was by far the "most unusual" question she'd ever heard at a meeting and that she'd never heard such a sentiment expressed by anyone wishing to adopt a child. She then advised the Noes to spend the next couple of days reevaluating their motives for adoption before contacting the bureau again.

But if the sister had definite misgivings, Arthur and Marie were convinced that they'd come across as exemplary parents. The very next day they wrote a follow-up letter, affirming their sincere desire to adopt a child, utilizing Cathy's death to reinforce their case.

The typewritten note, capitalized throughout and hand-signed by both of them, read: "AS WE SIT HERE WE PAUSE FOR A MOMENT TO THINK OF HOW MUCH WE LOVED OUR CHILD . . . EVEN FOR THE SHORT TIME. WE HAVE NOT GIVEN UP HOPE OF BEING PARENTS TO SOME CHILD."

On May 1, 1966, the Noes sent another letter to the bureau, enclosing black-and-white Polaroid photographs of themselves. In the letter, also capitalized, they apologized at great length that the picture was in black-and-white, saying that they had been unable to borrow a color Polaroid camera for the occasion.

On their adoption application the Noes listed Dr. Halbert Fillinger as a reference to their good character, although his only personal experience of the family was performing Mary Lee's autopsy. When Sister Michael Marie telephoned to inquire about Marie Noe, Dr. Fillinger told her succinctly: "Either she deserves a baby more than anyone else in the world, because she's lost so many kids, or she'll kill it real quick!"

Over the next two months, Arthur and Marie waited and waited for news from the Catholic Children's Bureau. As they became increasingly frustrated, they even considered accepting one of the many offers from pregnant women around the country. For in the wake of the publicity surrounding the deaths of their children, the Noes had received half-a-dozen letters from expectant mothers begging them to adopt their yet-unborn babies after reading about their plight.

But their initial excitement and willingness to do so was somewhat dampened by their attorney, Daniel Maxymuik, after he warned them that the natural mother could legally reclaim her baby at any time.

"We couldn't stand that," Marie Noe told him, saying that they were now pinning their hopes on the Catholic Children's Bureau. "We want to do it the right way."

TEN

A BLEEDING CHORUS

Although the Philadelphia Medical Examiner's official line was that Cathy had died a "typical" crib death, many of his colleagues were convinced it was simple murder. Dr. Robert Catherman had arrived in Philadelphia in the mid-60s to work as an assistant medical examiner and was on duty when Cathy Noe's corpse was brought in for autopsy.

Remembers Dr. Catherman: "My first entree to the whole thing was somebody saying, 'Oh, Jesus! Marie killed another one!' And I said, 'What does that mean? What's going on?' "

So his new colleagues proceeded to tell him that Cathy was just the latest in a series of dead Noe babies passing through the office. Although everybody was convinced they had a serial murderer running loose in Philadelphia, the autopsies provided no definite proof.

"We medical examiners were like a bleeding chorus," said Dr. Catherman. "But they chose not to listen to us."

Another young medical examiner in the office, Dr. Dimitri Contostavlos, said they were powerless to take action on circumstantial evidence alone.

"If you suspect a mother has suffocated her kid in that most private of relationships, you're not going to put her on the rack and torture her," he explained. "You're not going to find out. I've known mothers who have lain on their kids during sleep and they don't even know they've killed them. How are you ever going to prove murder? There's no signs."

Spelman's chief investigator Joe McGillen was only too well aware of these problems and had begun to search for a motive. His previous job had been investigating claims for a life insurance company and now he began concentrating on the policies the Noes had taken out on the lives of their babies.

From his own experience McGillen knew that parents often took out life insurance policies on their children. But he couldn't help wondering how a family that couldn't even afford their milk bill had so many brand-new appliances in their home.

McGillen's research revealed that the Noes had insured the lives of all but one of the babies that had died in unexplained circumstances. And they had already received thousands of dollars in payouts from insurance companies.

Three weeks after Cathy's death McGillen wrote confidential letters to the claims managers at the Sun Life Insurance Company and the Prudential Life Insurance Company, who had paid out policies on the Noe babies. He informed them that the Noes were under "intensive investigation," requesting full details of all the policies and payments made as soon as possible.

"While it would be premature at this time to conclude that any of these deaths are the result of foul play," wrote McGillen, "this consideration certainly cannot and isn't being overlooked."

He also asked them to advise the medical examiner's office in the event of Arthur and Marie applying for any death claim benefits on Cathy. McGillen didn't have

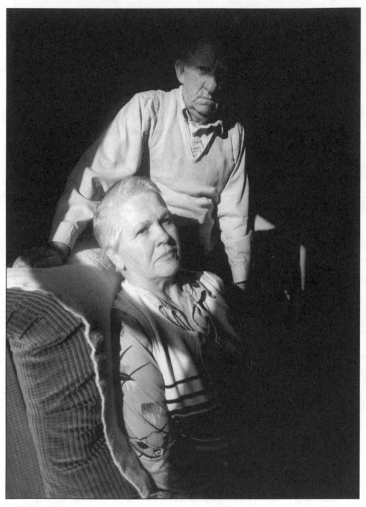

Arthur and Marie Noe at their Kensington home in January 1998. Three months after this picture was taken, Marie would finally confess to killing eight of her ten children.

(COURTESY *PHILADELPHIA DAILY NEWS* / SYGMA)

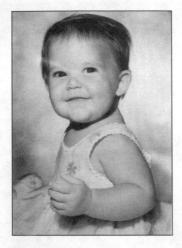

Cathy, the ninth Noe baby, who survived longer than any of her brothers or sisters. Spending much of her short life in the hospital, Cathy was a favorite of the nuns who nursed her. (COURTESY *PHILADELPHIA DAILY NEWS*/SYGMA)

Little Arty, the last of the Noe babies to die, was given lots of stuffed toys for Christmas 1967. A few weeks later he would die in his mother's care. (COURTESY *PHILADELPHIA DAILY NEWS*/SYGMA)

Marie and Arthur Noe regularly attended St. Hugh's Church, around the corner from their home. (COURTESY JOHN GLATT)

Forensic pathologist and coroner Dr. Halbert Fillinger, who became intrigued by the Marie Noe case after performing Mary Lee Noe's autopsy in the early 1960s. (COURTESY JOHN GLATT)

The Noes. After half a century of Marie's lies, the pain of his children's deaths is etched into the face of Arthur Noe. (COURTESY DAVID FIELDS/ SYGMA)

In February 1998 Marie and Arthur Noe invited a photographer to accompany them to New Cathedral Cemetery to visit some of their children's graves. (COURTESY DAVID FIELDS/SYGMA)

The Noes regularly made the pilgrimage to New Cathedral Cemetery, where the final remains of many of their babies lie. (COURTESY DAVID FIELDS/SYGMA)

Marie Noe fondly holds her favorite picture of her ninth baby, Cathy, who she murdered in February 1966. (COURTESY DAVID FIELDS/SYGMA)

The dilapidated house on N. American Street – where the Noes moved after little Arty's death in 1968 – will be Marie's prison until the day she dies. (COURTESY JOHN GLATT)

Marie and Arthur Noe spend their final days under siege in their run down home in Kensington. The conditions of Marie's bail mean she can never set foot outside the front door without police permission. (COURTESY DAVID FIELDS/ SYGMA)

After Marie's arrest for murder in late 1998, Arthur Noe went to pieces and contemplated buying a gun to kill himself. (COURTESY DAVID FIELDS/SYGMA)

Marie Noe's last two children, Cathy and Little Arty, share a grave in New Cathedral Cemetery. (COURTESY DAVID FIELDS/SYGMA)

long to wait. Within days of her death the Noes asked the Southwestern Insurance Company of Dallas to pay out the $1,500 policy they had taken out on her life.

The company flatly refused and returned their premium. The reason given for denying the claim was that the Noes had filled out a fraudulent application which had omitted their previous family history. Additionally, the insurance agent, referred to Arthur by a political contact after another company had refused their initial application, claimed to have seen Cathy at home when the policy was written on September 24, 1965, although she had been hospitalized at the time.

On hearing the news Arthur Noe flew into a fury and immediately appealed the decision through his friend and lawyer, Daniel Maxymuik. When he was subsequently interviewed by an insurance fraud investigator, the policy salesman swore he had seen the child twice on the two separate occasions he had visited the Noes. He told the investigator that the Noes must have provided another child in Cathy's place.

As there was no conclusive proof either way, the Southwestern Insurance Company of Dallas finally agreed to settle for $500. And when McGillen heard about the settlement he carefully noted it in his growing report on the Noes.

McGillen's theory that insurance fraud might be the key he was looking for was further strengthened after Sister Michael Marie informed him about Arthur Noe's concern over whether he would be able to insure an adopted child.

Two months after sending the black-and-white Polaroid pictures to the Catholic Adoption bureau, Marie and Arthur had heard nothing and were getting impatient. Eventually, they couldn't stand it any longer and arrived at the bureau, offering in the meantime to take in a foster child. Sister Michael Marie tactfully told them it would be better to wait and let their adoption application take its course. Then she telephoned Joe McGillen.

On July 1, 1966, Philadelphia *Bulletin* reporter Daniel J. McKenna was sent to interview the Noes and see how they were coping with their tragedy. Marie and Arthur welcomed him into the house, using the opportunity to attack the Catholic Archdiocese of Philadelphia for "dragging its feet."

When McKenna arrived the Noes were with two elders of the Mormon Church, whom they introduced as Lynn Reeder and John Glenn. After they left Arthur and Marie said how disappointed they were at not being given an adopted child, making no effort to mask their anger.

"All I can do is hope and pray," Marie told McKenna. "[They] gave us a lot of hope. We thought they might turn us down because we lost so many children. But [Sister Michael Marie] didn't think so."

Arthur Noe tried to be reasonable, saying that he realized there had to be an investigation before they could get a baby.

"But we get so anxious at times, especially Marie," he said. "We're hoping they'll give us a little girl, about two years old."

At that point Arthur left the room, returning a minute later with several color photographs of their daughter Cathy.

"Look how healthy she was," he declared with pride as his wife looked on with a blank smile.

When Sister Michael Marie read the subsequent story in the *Bulletin*'s Sunday edition where the Noes had criticized her agency, she was furious and immediately telephoned the medical examiner's office to complain. The sister has long since left the Philadelphia Catholic Social Services to join an order in Puerto Rico, but her former colleague, Sister Mary Frances, remembers the case. She says the bureau had decided at the beginning that Marie Noe would never get a baby from them, but they had to go through the proper adoption procedures.

"Her background was known," she recalled in 1998. "We got some negative vibes from her so there was no chance she was going to get a baby. I remember the sisters discussing that after what had happened to her, anyone would be hesitant to give her another baby."

The following March, Marie Noe arrived at the adoption bureau in a jubilant mood, announcing that she was pregnant again. She seemed ecstatically happy, telling Sister Michael Marie that she would no longer be requiring an adopted baby and was withdrawing her application.

The sister was amazed by the complete transformation in Marie's whole demeanor. Her previous moroseness had now been replaced by a new exuberance, as she announced her good news to the bewilderment of the nuns. Even her appearance was different. She had replaced her old clothes with a new outfit and had even visited the beauty parlor for a new hairdo.

As soon as she left, a concerned Sister Michael Marie called Joe McGillen, who contacted Dr. Columbus Gangemi to confirm the daunting news.

"Yes, unfortunately, I'm afraid that's true!" replied the doctor sadly.

Gangemi told McGillen that all his experiences with Marie Noe had emotionally drained him. He said he desperately wanted to wash his hands of the Noe family but Marie had already asked him to provide obstetric care for her tenth baby.

"[Isn't] there something you people could do about this?" he asked McGillen, saying he would be glad of any help to "relieve him of the responsibility."

When Dr. Spelman was told about Marie's newest pregnancy and Dr. Gangemi's frustrations, he stepped in to try and draw up a managed care program to monitor the mother's progress before and after the birth. He immediately contacted the director of the Maternal & Infant Care Project in the Philadelphia Department of Health, who agreed to help.

Somehow Marie Noe had managed to outsmart everyone by becoming pregnant again at the age of thirty-eight, but nobody had the slightest doubt of the fate that awaited the innocent baby now growing inside her.

ELEVEN

LITTLE ARTY

Arthur Joseph Noe was born at St. Joseph's Hospital on Friday, July 28, 1967, at 9:57 p.m., a battery of doctors standing by to make sure nothing went wrong. It was a difficult birth by cesarean section, complicated by the rupture of Marie Noe's uterine wall. Prior to birth her obstetric surgeon Dr. Salvatore Cucinotta had warned of likely complications under anesthesia, and she had signed a consent form to have her uterus removed in an emergency.

"I had to perform a severe hysterectomy on her," recalled Dr. Cucinotta, now eighty-seven years old and retired.

Although this was the third Noe baby Dr. Cucinotta had delivered, he was never informed that his patient was under investigation. Indeed, he had become so concerned about Marie's state of mind that he begged her to stop having children after Cathy's death. He even consulted a lawyer to discuss the legal implications of reporting his fears to the police, but he believed his hands were tied by medical ethics.

Ultimately, the only person he confided in was Dr. Gangemi, who had initially referred Marie Noe as a patient. And it was decided to ask the head of pediatrics at St. Joseph's, Dr. Patrick Pasquariello, to attend the delivery in case of birth trauma.

After delivery Dr. Cucinotta handed the new-born baby to Dr. Pasquariello, who carried it down the hall to the nursery for close observation. Little Arty, as the Noes called him, weighed eight pounds, five ounces at birth and was pronounced completely healthy by the doctors.

"There were no complications at delivery," observed Dr. Gangemi. "[He] was taken to the nursery in good condition."

The pediatric staff at St. Joseph's knew all about the other Noe babies, and would spend the next two months anxiously watching to make sure nothing went wrong. To their astonishment, Marie and Arthur Noe never once visited the baby they had so desperately wanted, during his long stay in the hospital. But even if his parents were ignoring him, the doctors at St. Joseph's were in constant attendance, giving him a barrage of tests to ensure that he remained healthy.

They kept a highly detailed hospital log, charting Little Arty's daily progress at St. Joseph's.

"The child appears normal in every respect," reported Dr. Gangemi. "NEVER has this child displayed any . . . respiratory embarrassment [as] described by his mother [in] her other deceased infants."

At ten days Little Arty was circumcised without complications. His color was good and he was eating well, noted his doctors. At the beginning of September there was a slight scare when the baby's hemoglobin levels began falling for no apparent reason, but doctors soon stabilized his blood levels and subsequent tests would reveal no abnormality.

On September 29th a reluctant Dr. Gangemi signed Little Arty's discharge note. Once again the frustrated family practitioner had deep reservations about letting a Noe baby go home, fearing a fate similar to those of his brothers and sisters. But all he could legally do was record his apprehensions for posterity in the official discharge note.

"A very close watch will be maintained on this child's development," he pledged. "In God we trust!"

A month later on October 30th Dr. Gangemi's fears were realized when St. Christopher's telephoned with the news that Little Arty, now three months old, was back in the hospital. He had been brought in by the rescue squad, limp, listless and pale. As usual Marie Noe had a ready explanation. She had been alone in the house feeding him when "something must have gone down the wrong way." When he began choking and turning blue, she had "banged it out of his chest," called the rescue squad and given mouth-to-mouth resuscitation until they came.

On arrival Little Arty appeared well nourished and in no apparent distress. But Dr. Gangemi insisted he be admitted to St. Joseph's Hospital anyway.

Once again the tiny baby was subjected to every conceivable test the doctors could think of; but all they could find was a slight cold. Throughout Little Arty's nineteen-day hospital stay his mother only visited him once, and that was when she was called in by an administrator to discuss a bill. Arthur Noe never once set foot in the hospital to see his son.

"Neither parent showed much interest in visiting this child," wrote a doctor when the baby was discharged on October 17th.

Five weeks later at 11:00 a.m. on December 21, the

police brought Little Arty into St. Joseph's emergency room in a terrible state. This time he had scratch marks on his face. Doctors managed to use oxygen to relieve a mild cyanosis and before long the baby's pale color returned to normal as he became alert again.

Marie Noe's explanation for the incident simply defied credibility. She said she had walked into his bedroom to find Little Arty crying and turning blue with the family cat lying across his face.

Dr. Charles Reed, the E.R. doctor on duty who saw Little Arty, was convinced it was no accident and wrote in his report: "POSSIBLE ATTEMPTED SUFFOCATION."

Yet the baby was allowed to go straight home so that Dr. Gangemi could see him that afternoon.

Christmas was four days later and Arthur and Marie staged a family celebration as they had done with Cathy two years earlier. They placed tiny Santa Claus figures around the front window and trimmed a Christmas tree in the front room, taping seasonal cards from friends and family around an archway leading to the dining room.

Little Arty's stocking was displayed on the living room wall, suspended from a wooden cross that a family friend had carved in Cathy's memory. It was filled to the brim with an assortment of stuffed animals, including teddy bears, a cow and a giraffe.

Arthur Noe would later tell police that it had been the best Christmas of his life. And he added that in his opinion Marie grew more beautiful each time she became pregnant.

But their celebrations were short-lived when Marie rushed Little Arty to Dr. Gangemi's office right after Christmas, running a temperature of 102 degrees. All the weary family physician could do was give the five-month-old, fifteen-pound baby a prescription to clear up the fever and send him home again. It would be the last time he would ever see Little Arty alive.

By New Year's Day, Little Arty's fever had subsided but he was starting to teethe, becoming cranky because of the pain. His father went to a drug store to buy Orajel and after rubbing it over his gums the baby stopped crying and fell asleep.

The following morning the baby woke up hungry at 6:30 a.m. and consumed a whole bottle of milk. After doing her daily self-hypnosis exercises Marie prepared breakfast for Arthur before he left for work.

At 10:00 a.m. she gave her baby son another bottle and he fell asleep. Ninety minutes later he awoke and started crying because his gums were hurting again. Marie took Little Arty downstairs to the parlor and after placing him in a chair to watch television, he calmed down.

A few minutes later she prepared his lunch, consisting of carrots, apricots and another bottle of milk. After he finished eating she took him back upstairs and put him to bed. Then she took a bath and went to sleep in the front bedroom.

At about 2:30 p.m. she awoke and checked on Little Arty, who was still sleeping peacefully, and went downstairs to the kitchen to prepare a chicken for Arthur's supper.

"I heard the crib rattling," Marie would tell homicide detectives a couple of hours later. "And although the baby was not crying, I went upstairs to check on him. The baby was lying in his crib, face up, gasping for breath and turning blue."

She claimed she then lowered the side of the crib, picked up Little Arty and started mouth-to-mouth resuscitation. When he failed to respond she returned him to the crib and dashed into the front bedroom to summon the rescue squad. Then she called her husband at work.

Running back into the baby's room, she plucked Little Arty out of his crib, wrapped him in a blanket and brought him downstairs.

"I placed him on the kitchen table," she would later tell detectives, "and started mouth-to-mouth resuscitation again."

A few minutes later the rescue squad arrived and rushed Little Arty to St. Christopher's Hospital, where he was declared dead on arrival at 4:10 p.m.

In her 1998 confession Marie Noe could recall little of the events the day her tenth and last child died.

"I can't remember if I hurt him or not," was her feeble reply when was asked if she had injured him.

Rem Bristow was on late afternoon duty that Tuesday at the medical examiner's office when the hospital called with news of Little Arty's untimely death. His first reaction was that it was murder and he telephoned the Philadelphia Homicide Squad, asking them to investigate.

At 7:30 that evening homicide Detective Vincent Toner and Sergeant John Donnelly arrived at 3447 N. American Street and read Arthur and Marie Noe their legal rights off a standard police interrogation card.

"I have nothing to hide," declared Marie confidently, saying she didn't need a lawyer present. "I will tell you everything I can possibly remember."

She then related details of Little Arty's various medical ailments and hospitalizations, giving her account of the way he died. On their way out she told the detectives that they were welcome to call anytime."

Arthur Noe could add little to Marie's statement except to wipe his tearful eyes and say: "I have no idea why this is always happening to us. I wish to God I did."

The following morning Philadelphia awoke to the stunning news that the tenth Noe baby had died in unexplained circumstances. Under the headline "Couple's 10th Child Is Taken By Death," the *Philadelphia Daily News* described in wrenching detail how tragedy had once again struck the Noes' modest Kensington row home.

"Ten children . . . ten children . . . and every one of them gone. One at a time," it began.

"The story of Arthur and Marie Noe and their children is as unbelievably tragic as it is mysterious. For there is no cure for heartbreak, nor an answer to death.

"Their tenth child—five-month-old Arthur J.—died as swiftly and mysteriously as had his nine little brothers and sisters in the years before. What is it causing the deaths? The Noes, numbed by the latest shock, are as baffled as pathologists from coast to coast."

After the homicide detectives had left the night before, Arthur and Marie welcomed reporters into their tiny living room, as they sadly packed up their Christmas ornaments.

Still wearing the warehouseman uniform he had put on that morning to go to work, Arthur, now forty-seven and balding, looked stunned with shock, the deep furrows under his eyes making him appear many years older. A tearful Marie, dressed in a plain cotton dress, seemed numb and totally oblivious to the commotion, as she began taking down the Christmas cards over the archway.

"Please," Arthur appealed to a reporter. "We don't want to say anything. We have too much in our hearts. We had too much publicity before and we don't want to go through that again."

But as the reporters started firing questions at him, Arthur composed himself and assumed his public pose.

"I don't have anything to say at this time and I'll tell you why," he continued. "We have just been through this so many times ... It's just heartbreak, just heartbreak."

On Wednesday morning Dr. Molly Dapena performed an autopsy on Little Arty with Dr. Marvin Aaronson, but found nothing. Yet again the cause of death was officially ruled "not determined," with the manner of death "unknown."

"There are no reasons to believe that [the deaths] are not natural," medical examiner Dr. Joseph Spelman told the press after the autopsy, in a deliberate attempt to quell the growing rumors of murder. "From a medical point of view there is absolutely nothing at this time. This is no different from the findings on the other children."

But Spelman added that the dead baby's tissues would be examined by his laboratory to see if they could shed any additional light on his death.

Although Arthur and Marie Noe had initially been reluctant to discuss their horrible plight, by the next morning they seemed only too happy to be interviewed. And as Little Arty's body was sliced open by pathologists, they were taping several television interviews that would air later that evening.

Soon after the television crews left, Joseph McGillen of the medical examiner's office arrived. Arthur immediately recognized him from the time he had questioned them after Cathy's death. This time McGillen tried to be as sympathetic as possible, paying his condolences and saying how sorry he had been to hear about Little Arty's death.

The seasoned investigator then engaged them in a conversational manner to relax them so they were off-guard. Then he hoped they might let something slip which could be used later in the investigation.

Sympathizing with their loss, McGillen said it must be hard having to deal with the press in such difficult circumstances. He asked them if they had gotten much peace from the media during this trying time. Marie replied that they hadn't but they realized that the reporters had a job to do, so they were being patient. They said they hoped these television interviews would be the end of it so they could get on with their lives.

Then, attempting to feed their obvious love of publicity, McGillen explained that being "celebrities" and "unique in the history of medicine," their story was of national and even international interest. And he warned them to expect overtures from the television networks for a documentary on their experiences.

"Their reaction to this was amazing," McGillen wrote in his subsequent OME report. "Their faces registered their sudden interest in knowing more about the possibilities of this happening."

Later, when McGillen tried to steer the interview to other matters, an excited Arthur Noe kept returning to the possibilities of television, asking for advice on how he should handle it. The canny investigator told them that *he* would base his decision on the facts; that their children were dead and could never be brought back.

"I said I would consider whether or not I cared what friends and relatives might think for what would be seen on my part to be a commercialization of [their children's] deaths."

Arthur appeared delighted with the possible new money-making opportunities opening up before his eyes, eagerly inviting McGillen to come back and discuss it further.

A week later Arthur and Marie were the focus of a second article in *Newsweek*. It was a follow-up to the story the magazine had run on the Noes in March 1966, after Cathy's death. This time the Noes were used to illustrate and humanize what was now being seen as a national SIDS epidemic.

"Doctors could only offer consolation but not understanding of what had taken the lives of their children," said the *Newsweek* article. "Arthur Jr., like at least four other Noe children—and an estimated 15,000 to 25,000 other infants each year—died without any signs of fatal illness or other apparent cause. The cause or causes of these 'crib deaths' continue to mystify pathologists and pediatricians."

Although secretly convinced that Marie Noe had murdered her children, Philadelphia Medical Examiner Dr. Joseph Spelman told *Newsweek* that he had found nothing to indicate unnatural death.

"There has been no positive progress in explaining crib deaths," said the medical examiner. "Only exploded theories."

For the medical examiner and the doctors acquainted with the Noe case, the only good news was that Marie Noe could never become a natural mother again after her radical hysterectomy.

PART TWO

GETTING AWAY WITH MURDER

TWELVE

THE INVESTIGATION

It was a freezing Sunday evening on January 7, 1968, when Arthur and Marie Noe held a public viewing for Little Arty's body at the Wildey Funeral Home. A couple of days earlier Arthur Noe had called the *Philadelphia Daily News* and asked them to publicize it. A brief announcement had run in the Saturday edition.

By the time OME investigator Rem Bristow arrived at the funeral home at 8:30 p.m., Arthur and Marie Noe were standing by the tiny casket wearing their customary black mourning outfits. Several rows behind were the dead baby's grandfather James Lyddy, talking to Marie's sister Anne Danielski and her husband Stanley. As canned organ music played through the public address system, several curiosity seekers arrived, hoping for a first-hand look at America's most famous bereaved parents.

When Joe McGillen walked in at 8:40 p.m. Arthur and Marie both clasped his hand, as if greeting an old friend. The investigator noted that Marie seemed exceptionally tense standing so close to her dead baby's body.

A few minutes later they joined McGillen on a pew at the back of the room. Arthur did most of the talking as Marie constantly wrung her hands together, as if in distress. He said how nice everybody had been in their time of need, especially his boss at Zurn Industries, who had given him tomorrow off for Little Arty's funeral. He planned to return to work on Tuesday, he told McGillen, as his biggest problem was having too much time on his hands to think.

"I can't understand why this always keeps happening to us," he kept repeating in his throaty, smoker's voice. "I suppose it is God's will."

At one point McGillen asked Marie what she would do when Arthur returned to work. Immediately she became animated as if a switch had suddenly been turned on in her head, replying that she would love to do volunteer work but Arthur wouldn't allow it.

Then she startled the investigator with the news that she intended to reactivate her application to the Catholic Children's Bureau for an adopted child, as she could no longer have her own.

"No! No!" Arthur suddenly chimed in. "Maybe in a couple of years when we get straightened out, but not now."

Then she suggested trying for a foster child instead.

"No!" shouted Arthur again, turning red with anger. "I don't want to think about any more children for a good while yet."

Then, calming down, he congratulated the Philadelphia police on how they had questioned them at home, instead of locking them up behind bars and grilling them like they had when Mary Lee died.

"He was going stir-crazy," commented Marie.

At 10:00 a.m. the following morning a Mass of the Angels was offered for Little Arty at St. Hugh's Church. Then Arthur and Marie led the mourners a few blocks away to the New Cathedral Cemetery to bury their tenth and last baby.

*   *   *

Three days after Little Arty's death, Dr. Joseph Spelman received an intriguing telephone call from the Noes' estranged friend Linda Harris. She told the medical examiner that after reading the newspaper accounts of the baby's death, she had vital information on the Noes that she could no longer keep to herself. After a promise from Spelman to keep her identity confidential, she agreed to meet with Joe McGillen later that day at her home in Kensington.

The story that the pseudonymous Linda Harris told McGillen was the big break he had been praying for. The dogged investigator listened intently as she detailed her twenty-seven-year friendship with Arthur Noe, which had begun when they were neighbors; a full seven years before he had met Marie.

She outlined Arthur's miserable childhood and how he had felt unloved and unwanted until nineteen-year-old Marie Lyddy had seduced him. An eyewitness to their first meeting at the Coopersville Singing Club, Doris watched as the young girl with the reputation of being "boy-crazy" completely overwhelmed the inexperienced twenty-seven-year-old, who was a full head shorter.

In hushed whispers Linda told McGillen about the early years of the Noe marriage and the constant arguments she'd witnessed during her frequent visits to their home.

"She helped Marie care for the first three children," noted McGillen in his report. "In her judgment they all appeared at all times to be perfectly healthy and normal."

Linda also revealed that it was an open secret in the

neighborhood that Marie was interested in other men, as Arthur was unable to satisfy her demands for sex. Although remaining close to the Noes, Linda told McGillen she and others had not believed Marie's story of being raped while seven months pregnant with her first baby.

At first when the babies had begun dying, Linda had believed it had been natural. But she soon changed her mind in May 1952 after Jacqueline died and Marie temporarily went blind.

"[She] begun to grow very suspicious of Marie," observed McGillen. "The suspicions were fed by Marie's own peculiar behavior."

By 1954 Linda and her husband began to distance themselves from the Noes, deliberately cutting down on their visits. They became convinced there was something wrong with Marie and questioned if the deaths of her babies had been accidental.

But it would take another ten years for Linda Harris to become certain, with the death of Mary Lee, that Marie was killing her babies. Several times she considered going to the medical examiner but always decided against it, not wanting to break the neighborhood code by interfering in other people's business. But after reading about the death of Little Arty, she finally decided the time had come to break her silence.

When McGillen reported back to Dr. Spelman they decided it was time for the police to step up their ongoing investigation into the Noes. Additionally, Spelman ordered McGillen to work full-time on the investigation and find some answers.

*   *   *

On January 10, Dr. Spelman's chief investigator James McGovern telephoned the commander of the Philadelphia Homicide Division, Captain E. Zongolowicz, who agreed to participate in a joint investigation with the medical examiner's office. He assigned Detective Joseph Schimpf from his unsolved crimes division, Five Squad, to head it.

"The captain called me over and introduced me to Joe McGillen, who was just leaving his office," remembers Detective Schimpf, now retired after twenty-two years' service with the Philadelphia Police Department.

"He told me he was working on a woman who had ten baby deaths and asked me to go out with him."

Schimpf quickly acquainted himself with the Marie Noe case by reading McGillen's hand-written report of the investigation so far. It was agreed that Detective Schimpf would carry out his own investigation in tandem with McGillen and Bristow's. Together and separately they would interview everyone who knew the Noes.

Right from the start there was friction between the experienced homicide detective and what he viewed as amateurs from the medical examiner's office.

"I think McGillen was a newspaper hound," says Schimpf today. "He was very passionate about solving the case and let it be known that he was going to write a book about this woman."

Over the next few weeks the investigators scoured the streets of Kensington, questioning the Noes' family, friends and neighbors. Arthur and Marie were fully aware that they were under intense surveillance and were even followed on several occasions.

One night Arthur Noe spotted a plain-clothes detective sitting at the bar of his local taproom and decided to play a trick on him.

"I said to Marie, 'That's the detective from the 25th precinct,' " Arthur told *Philadelphia Magazine* writer Stephen Fried. "So I said to the bartender, 'Jack, do you have a Polaroid camera?' "

When the bartender pulled one out from under the bar Arthur told him to buy the detective a drink and snap a photograph of him, saying, "That's from Mr. and Mrs. Noe." According to Arthur the embarrassed detective left the bar immediately and never returned.

THIRTEEN

DOOR TO DOOR

On Friday, January 12th, 1968, the investigation gathered momentum when Detective Schimpf interviewed Arthur Noe's cousin, Helen Harper. They met at her home on Greene Street, in Philadelphia, where she initially declared that she didn't want to get involved in other people's business. But gradually she warmed up to the experienced detective's questioning.

She told Schimpf she had always thought the deaths of the Noe babies were "fishy," as on each occasion Marie had been home alone with them. Mrs. Harper also mentioned Marie's strange behavior, citing an occasion when Marie had disappeared to Florida for a couple of days.

"Arthur doesn't like anyone to know about this," she confided. "He would be furious if he knew I was telling [you] about it."

When Schimpf asked her about the first alleged rape, she replied it seemed "mighty funny" that Marie's father-in-law had been in the house at the time it was supposed to have happened.

The following morning, Detective Schimpf spoke to Marie's oldest sister, Helen Mills, at her home on Williams Avenue in the Philadelphia suburb of Cedarbrook. Although only living a couple of miles away from her younger sister, she said she never saw the Noes and didn't bother with them.

Mrs. Mills also thought it peculiar that Marie had lost so many babies. But after she read about the SIDS death of President Kennedy's son, Patrick, she stopped thinking it could be unnatural. Although not having any personal experience of Marie as a mother, she had been told by other members of the family that the babies were always well-fed and taken care of.

Detective Schimpf then drove east to Parkwood Manor on the borders of Bucks County to interview Marie's younger brother John Lyddy. The once-troubled boy was now in his late thirties and married. John readily admitted being a loner, saying he didn't have much to do with his family.

When asked about his sister's earliest alleged rape in 1949, John said that although he was in the service at the time he did remember Marie being sexually assaulted by a coast guard on an earlier occasion, during a family vacation in Cape May, New Jersey.

John and his wife both agreed that Marie was a quiet, secretive person who kept things to herself. Neither thought there was anything suspicious about her losing so many babies.

After lunch Detective Schimpf drove south to Webb Street, Kensington, to meet with Marie's sister, Anne Danielski, whom she always called "Sis." Although she lived just a few streets away, Anne said that she hadn't seen her sister in more than six years.

Describing Marie as "a little slow" but certainly "not stupid," Anne said that Marie was a hard worker who liked children. Although she was never suspicious of the deaths of her nieces and nephews, she remarked it was odd that Arthur was never home when they occurred.

The following Tuesday morning Joe McGillen and Rem Bristow began their part of the investigation. Acting on a tip from Linda Harris, they went to see Iona Fisher, who had been a friend of the Lyddys for many years. The interview was cut short when Fisher insisted she could tell them "nothing about those people," although she admitted knowing Marie and Arthur for many years.

McGillen and Bristow's next stop was Florence Hilton, whose son Ronnie was married to Geraldine Lyddy, the illegitimate baby who was a dark family secret and had been brought up as Marie's sister. Initially reluctant to talk to the investigators, for fear of "getting involved in their affairs," Mrs. Hilton described the Lyddys as "a strange family," estranged from each other. She said the family believed that Marie's problems with the babies dated back to her near-fatal bout of scarlet fever as an infant.

Living in the Noes' neighborhood at N. Bodine Street, she was well acquainted with the gossip surrounding the baby deaths. She said she had frequently seen Marie pushing different babies around in their carriages over the years and the children never seemed ill-treated or abused.

That afternoon McGillen and Bristow drove to N. American Street to interview Sophie Curry, who lived directly opposite the Noes with her daughter. Mrs. Curry said that Marie and Arthur kept to themselves and were close to no one in the neighborhood. She too had seen Marie pushing her babies around Kensington on occasion and they had always appeared healthy and well-dressed.

Asked about the Noes as neighbors, Mrs. Curry said that Arthur Noe was a heavy drinker who often drank to excess. She had seen him drunk regularly, staggering home from his favorite bar at Philip and Tioga Streets, but had never seen Marie inebriated. She also mentioned that the Noes had been the subject of much talk in the neighborhood when they were seen happily drinking at the bar immediately after the death of one of their babies.

Mrs. Curry said that in her opinion Marie should be psychoanalyzed because "they've tried everything else and they don't know why the babies died." She added that everyone in the neighborhood wondered how a family could lose so many children in unexplained circumstances. But the general feeling was that the babies had died in a series of tragic occurrences that was beyond their understanding. After all, if the authorities couldn't explain why the babies died, how could they?

After McGillen and Bristow left Mrs. Curry's house they walked around N. American Street, seeking anyone who knew the Noes, however distantly. A few doors down the street they met a young married couple, Patricia and Michael McMahon, who had moved into the neighborhood after they'd wed six months earlier.

Patricia first met Marie Noe the previous summer and still had not heard about her dead babies. She had been sitting on her front step talking to friends when Marie passed by with Little Arty in his carriage. Everyone started admiring the little baby, but Patricia thought Marie seemed strange and stand-offish. She never spoke unless asked a direct question, and even then she usually only replied "yes" or "no."

When somebody remarked that Little Arty looked just

like his sister Catherine, Marie looked surprised, replying, "Oh, do you really think so?"

A few days later Patricia said that she had been told the Noes' tragic history by her next-door neighbor Marion Bowyers, who had witnessed Little Arty being rushed to the hospital the previous October. According to Patricia, Mrs. Bowyers then commented, "Once they take them out the first time they never live after that."

Intrigued by the remark, the investigators went straight next door to interview Mrs. Bowyers, who seemed puzzled that they should be questioning her about the Noes. Going on the defensive, she said she didn't know them personally and therefore could not help their inquiry. She denied ever harboring the slightest suspicion against her neighbor, describing Marie as a good mother who would never harm her children.

"After all," she told the investigators, "when they do the autopsies, they don't find anything wrong with the children and even the doctors don't know why they die."

McGillen and Bristow did not bring up the negative comment attributed to her by Patricia McMahon.

That afternoon the OME detectives drove downtown to City Hall, where they had an appointment on the seventh floor with County Detective Buckenhorst of the district attorney's office. It was Detective Buckenhorst who had liaised with the medical examiner's office in their abortive joint investigation, after Mary Lee Noe's death in January 1963.

After getting the permission of his superior, Lieutenant Talmadge Jackson, he found the old files from the previous investigation and sat down with McGillen and Bristow to review them. They spent the afternoon poring through old newspaper clippings on the Noes and the OME investigators took copies.

The following day Detective Schimpf joined Mc-Gillen and Bristow to return to Kensington for more interviews. Both teams would make separate reports of what was said in these interviews, and there would be telling differences.

The three investigators first met with Rosella Heile-mann, whose N. Dillman Street home backs directly onto the Noes. Mrs. Heilemann said she saw little of the Noes at home as they always kept their shades drawn and that she didn't snoop.

Where Detective Schimpf later reported that Heile-mann described Marie's frequent failure to acknowledge long-time neighbors as "unintentional snubs," McGillen quoted her as using the word "strange."

"Sometimes [Marie] will say hello to you," McGillen later reported, "and other times she doesn't even seem to notice you."

The investigation then moved around the corner to N. Waterloo Street, where they had been wrongly told that another ex-neighbor, Grace Ross, had been godmother to one of the Noe babies. After explaining that it was in fact her step-sister, Lee Curran, who was the godparent, Mrs. Ross said she had met the family after buying her house from James Lyddy, but barely knew them.

Whereas Detective Schimpf wrote that Ross thought Marie Noe "a little slow," McGillen uses the words "somewhat mentally slow" in his version.

The next day they met up again to interview Violetta Zimba, the former next-door neighbor who had tried to save Constance's life in March 1958. With this interview the two investigative teams diverged onto completely different tracks.

While Schimpf's later report gives a vague thumbnail sketch of Violetta's dramatic arrival at the Noe home to discover Constance turning blue, McGillen's richly detailed one vividly describes Marie's total inability to comprehend the situation, as she and Arthur desperately try to revive the baby until the arrival of the emergency services.

"She just stood off to one side wringing her hands," Violetta is quoted as saying.

Detective Schimpf's version also fails to mention any of Violetta's revealing details of her personal observations on the Noes. For instance, when asked if she ever heard Arthur and Marie arguing, Violetta "smiled slightly and said she had."

The investigators then saw another Noe neighbor named Carrie McDonald, who knew the family from Arthur's frequent visits to her N. American Street home, collecting for St. Hugh's Church. Once again Detective Schimpf's report is brief and factual, without noting many of her observations on the Noes. He fails to mention how Mrs. McDonald believed it strange that Marie had lost so many babies and thought it would be a good idea "if they could be psychoanalyzed to see if there's anything wrong with either of them that way."

The two teams were also at some variance in separating gossip from fact, especially with Mrs. McDonald's anecdote of Marie and Arthur's inappropriate visit to a bar, so soon after the death of one of their babies.

Detective Schimpf's version reads: "They came around taking up a collection for the baby after it died, like they did for all the babies. The collector said he stopped in the bar and when he did he saw Arthur and Marie playing shuffleboard. Mrs. McDonald said she doesn't know this to be a fact, but only something she heard from the collector."

In the McGillen/Bristow report: "People in the neighborhood didn't like it a bit when, immediately following the death of one of their children, Marie and Arthur Noe were seen in the taproom around the corner shooting shuffleboard. [Mrs. McDonald] said they were observed thusly by those who were in the process of taking up a neighborhood collection for flowers. They had gone into this bar to solicit money there and found the Noes in there 'having a good time.' She said the burial of the baby hadn't yet taken place."

On leaving Mrs. McDonald, the investigators walked by 3447 N. American Street, where they saw Arthur and Marie, sitting together on a sofa in the front room watching television. They didn't stop and the Noes never noticed them.

Then they met with another neighbor, Doris Sincavage, who was there with her husband, a policeman attached to the 6th District, and young son. Mrs. Sincavage, who lived two doors away from the Noes, told them she had known the family since they first moved in. Although she had only met them on a few occasions, she thought they were wonderful people. But in her view the Noes were not the type of people you could get close to.

Questioned about Marie's babies, Mrs. Sincavage said she never suspected her neighbor of doing anything untoward, and was shocked that anyone could think such a bad thing.

"I trust her so much that I would even let her take care of my children, if I had any small ones," she told the investigators.

McGillen would later note that Mrs. Sincavage was typical of most of the neighbors, who based their comments on an unwillingness to believe that anyone could actually harm a child "rather than any factual first-hand knowledge of the Noes as parents or, for that matter, as individuals."

On Saturday morning the two teams met up again to interview Robert Valentine, the neighbor whom Doris Harris had claimed Marie Noe was in love with. But Joe McGillen, who was leading the questioning on this occasion, did not broach the subject as Valentine's wife and mother-in-law were also there.

Valentine told the investigators that he was a regular at the bar the Noes frequented and had known Marie since she was a child. He said that although they were not drunks, they certainly enjoyed an evening out.

At that point Valentine's mother-in-law because furious about him discussing the Noes, saying that she didn't want to meddle in other people's affairs. She put on her coat suddenly and stormed out of the front door, only to return a few moments later in a more composed state.

As the questioning continued, Valentine and his mother-in-law both recalled Marie's alleged rape in 1954, exactly nine months before the birth of her fourth baby. Valentine had been drinking in the corner bar when Arthur ran in, screaming that his wife had been raped and to call the police. He said nobody really believed Marie was telling the truth and thought she had made it up.

Recalling Marie as a teenager, Valentine said she certainly hadn't been wild and had stayed close to home as she often had to mind her younger sister Geraldine (who was in reality her niece). He found Marie very childish and slow and always thought it strange that she could have lost so many children in unexplained circumstances.

Suddenly his wife spoke up for the first time since they had arrived, saying: "How come if you people can't find anything wrong with the babies, you come around asking all these questions? What are we supposed to know if you people don't know what killed them?"

They then drove to Northeast Philadelphia to question Angelika Ciambrello, another ex-neighbor of the Noes. She had first heard about Marie's plight from other neighbors and recalled how the Noes used to sit out on their stoop with their two dogs and white cat. She said the neighborhood children used to gather around the front step to pet the animals and Marie and Arthur always seemed friendly to the children.

It was already getting dark when the investigators drove north to the Philadelphia suburb of Warminster to interview Marie's sister Frances and her husband Frank Stinson, who had grown up with Arthur. Although McGillen's report devotes almost three single-spaced pages to this interview, Detective Schimpf's is a mere fraction of that.

The Stinsons lived in a ramshackle house in a slum housing project on Adams Avenue. The investigators sat around the kitchen table as McGillen took charge, telling the Stinsons that they were investigating the deaths of Marie's babies for the medical examiner's office, carefully omitting that it was being viewed as possible homicide.

Wrote McGillen in his follow-up report: "I indicated that we have been very interested in these deaths and why they occur with such frequency and that, from a medical standpoint, the deaths are certainly puzzling and mysterious."

The Stinsons agreed to cooperate but said they had had little or no contact with Arthur and Marie Noe in the last five years.

"[My] family is like that," Frances Stinson told him. "We don't see any of the others too often."

She told the investigators about Marie's early life and how she had never fully recovered her mental faculties after the scarlet fever. Their parents, whom she described as "too strict," always kept a close watch on Marie and didn't allow her out much as a young girl, for fear of what might happen.

McGillen then asked her about her sister's temporary blindness after the death of her first baby. Frances said the doctors believed it had been caused by shock and was psychological. Afterward she had taken Marie to see a psychiatrist a couple of times but she had stopped the treatment, saying she could not afford the $25-a-session fee. Her husband added that later Marie had seen a psychiatrist at Temple Hospital.

The Stinsons both recalled the 1949 rape allegation.

"It was a terrible thing and it shook Marie up pretty bad," said Frances, who could not recall the second alleged rape in 1954. But her husband did, saying: "Yes, you do. You remember when [Arthur] came home and found her tied up."

For the first time since they arrived, Detective

Schimpf spoke up and asked about Marie's first allegation of rape as a young teenager in Cape May. But he immediately dropped the subject when it became clear that Frances did not wish to discuss it.

McGillen then questioned Frank Stinson about Arthur Noe, who had been a boyhood pal when they both attended Northeast Public High School. He said he knew nothing about Arthur and his brother Charles being placed in an orphanage and wasn't aware that Arthur had been seriously ill as a child.

But he did tell the investigators how they had both taken their army medicals together, with him passing and Arthur failing. When the babies began dying, he said, Marie had undergone several physical examinations to see what could be wrong, but Arthur had always refused to so. Stinson said he had often wondered if Arthur might have some physical problem which could account for the deaths of his children.

The interview finished with the Stinsons saying they did not suspect Arthur and Marie of causing their babies' death, adding that the autopsies should have revealed if there was anything wrong.

On a cold, wet Monday evening nine days later Arthur and Marie Noe arrived at Philadelphia's infamous Roundhouse police headquarters to be questioned about the deaths of their children. This time it was a police matter and Detective Schimpf and his colleague Detective James McGowan ran the interrogation.

The Noes were fully cooperative and both agreed to undergo polygraph tests. Marie was tested that day and Arthur three days later. Although under great pressure, well aware of the intense investigation into their lives, they seemed remarkably calm and collected, saying that they wouldn't be needing a lawyer.

Unlike Joe McGillen's 1963 interrogation, when he had separated them to prevent them from helping each other, Detective Schimpf allowed them to stay together so they would be more at ease. He had unwittingly given them an advantage.

Schimpf began by asking them to explain why Marie had always been alone with her babies. Arthur immediately repudiated this. He now claimed that others were home when several of the babies died, adding that his late brother Charles was present in February 1951, with the second Noe baby, Elizabeth. He boldly told detectives that the investigators from the medical examiner's office must have been mistaken.

Marie also altered some of her earlier accounts of her babies' deaths, telling detectives that in her opinion Cathy had still been alive when the emergency squad arrived to take her to the hospital. She also now claimed that the pet cat had never gotten into little Arty's playpen but had merely scratched his face.

She maintained that her babies had all been normal and healthy except for some "blood trouble." According to her, the doctors were well aware of it when they treated the children.

When asked about her incidents of blindness, Marie told the detectives that it had been the result of a spinal injection which had caused severe headaches, resulting in her temporary sight loss. She added that during her eye treatment she had been injected with a truth drug and asked about her children's deaths. Later the doctors told her she had nothing to fear as she hadn't said anything to incriminate herself.

When Detective Schimpf asked if she had ever suffered any mental lapses or blackouts, she and Arthur both denied that she had, although Marie admitted a possible mental lapse after the death of Arthur Jr., when she had been so "shaken up" that she had taken off for Florida one morning without telling anyone.

"[I] called Arthur from Jacksonville," she explained. "Then [I] took a bus back to Richmond, Va., where Arthur met me. You might call this a mental lapse or something but [I don't] because [I] knew what [I] was doing all the time. But [I] just don't know why I did it."

The Noes were then asked why they kept having children after losing so many. They replied they had both always wanted a family and that all the tests on Marie had proved negative so they had carried on. But they admitted there were times they felt "disgusted" but always talked it over and then tried for another baby.

"The fear was always there," said Arthur. "That's why Marie submitted to so many tests."

Arthur said that all his difficulties had led to him straying from the church on several occasions, but he had always returned. He emphasized that presently he was a good church member and did everything he could to help his parish.

The Noes were then questioned about Catherine Noe's life insurance policy, which had been found invalid as they hadn't revealed any of their children's previous deaths. Arthur now took the detectives into his confidence, claiming that the insurance salesman who visited the house was so desperate for business that he pretended he'd seen Cathy, even though she was in the hospital at the time. Arthur said he hadn't *exactly* lied to the salesman about not having other children. He had merely taken him literally, as he was never directly asked about any children prior to Cathy.

After Arthur and Marie both passed the polygraph test, Schimpf wrote that he was completely satisfied that they were telling the truth and "there was no deception noted."

Looking back at his interrogation today, the seventy-seven-year-old former detective, who is seriously ill with Parkinson's, stands by his report exonerating them.

"I just found them to be a normal couple at the time," he said from his Tennessee home in 1998. "Especially after I gave them the lie detector test and they both passed. No problems. So I didn't think there was any use me getting all excited over it."

Forensic pathologist Dr. Halbert Fillinger, who autopsied several Noe babies and had lectured at the FBI's legendary academy in Quantico, Virginia, says polygraph tests are not infallible.

"That's a serious mistake we have found," he explained. "Because if you have someone with a very flat affect the lie detector test doesn't work very well. Marie didn't seem to really recognize that she had done something to take [her babies'] lives."

Dr. Fillinger believes that the polygraph machine, which responds to changes in auditory stimuli, would not have been effective in this instance.

"One of the things that we always watch for in polygraphing someone is if they are able to respond to a stimulus or if they are just a total flat line. I think Marie Noe could have been a flat line."

On February 7, 1968, Detective Schimpf drafted his final twenty-one-page report, submitting it to his superior,

Captain Zongolowicz, with a copy to the medical examiner's office. It bore little resemblance to the richly detailed one by Joe McGillen and Rem Bristow. Schimpf's findings appear to deliberately undermine the OME investigators, whom he considered amateurs with "some warped ideas."

The detective was certainly handicapped by never interviewing Dr. Gangemi and the other doctors who had personally witnessed Marie Noe's behavior. But he believed that it would have been a waste of time to interview the doctors as the babies were always dead when they saw them.

He also failed to read the original police reports covering the deaths of the first five babies. Although they had been destroyed by the department nine years earlier, there were still copies readily available in the medical examiner's office. If he had he would have seen that Arthur Noe had never previously claimed to have been present when any of his children died.

Detective Schimpf's findings were as follows:

> The assigned, after interviewing Arthur and Marie Noe, found them to be just plain simple people, and although friendly, are somewhat withdrawn, but when talking to them they seem to go out of their way to be accepted.
>
> This is especially true of Arthur, who is active in civic affairs, is a committee man and also does church work. He is talkative and creates the impression that he likes to feel important.
>
> Marie, on the other hand, does not volunteer any conversation. She is pleasant and does however, reply eagerly to any questions and/or small

talk, but when answering you is hesitant for a second or two, as if thinking before speaking. She speaks with an air of average intelligence. She creates the impression in the assigned, that her reaction to a given set of circumstances would be somewhat slow or delayed.

The facts established by the assigned are as follows—

1) All the children at the time of birth were apparently healthy, except for the stillborn baby and the one that lived six hours.

2) All the children were clean and well-nourished and were well kept and cared for.

3) There is a history of the children from Arthur Jr. on to Arthur Joseph (#4 to 10) of being treated in the hospital one or more times for what Marie said was either shortness of breath or of turning blue.

4) When any of these children were found in difficulty, from information and records available, indications are that professional help was sought or administered.

5) The mother was not always home alone as previously reported or implied.

6) Records from the OME indicate that an inquest was held in deaths 1, 2 and 3 and where autopsies were performed, no cause or manner of death could be determined.

Detective Schimpf concluded that there was "no evidence of foul play present" and the case was closed. And since at that time it was the police and not the district attorney—future Republican Senator Arlen Specter—who decided whether or not to prosecute, Marie Noe would remain free for the next thirty years.

When Joe McGillen had told Dr. Spelman about his adoption discussion with Marie Noe at the funeral home, the medical examiner was livid. He determined the Noes would never get an innocent child through the system.

Although he was currently telling the media that he had no suspicions, privately he felt otherwise. And even though the investigation had been officially closed, he took the unprecedented step of writing two identical letters to block any future attempt by the Noes to adopt or foster a child.

One letter was addressed to the city office in charge of adoptions, foster home placements and child protection services. The other was to its state counterpart. These two letters would remain buried with Little Arty's autopsy report for three decades before being discovered in 1997. Then, finally, the long-dead medical examiner's true feelings about Marie Noe would be heard.

"You undoubtedly have read about the death of the tenth child in [the Noe] family," began the letters. "This office has actively investigated several of these deaths. We have extensive files on the background of this family. We are not willing to declare with certainty that these children died natural deaths.

"In the event that thought is given to placing children

under the care of the Noes, we would be glad to discuss our file and our thoughts in detail."

At that time Spelman had just three years to live. A recent battle with alcoholism had left him tired and weary. He also had a major scandal on his hands after his chief pathologist, Dr. Joseph Campbell, had been caught falsifying testimony in a case. Spelman had only just managed to save Campbell's job, but there had been a lot of adverse publicity, reflecting badly on the medical examiner's office.

"I know that Spelman had a lot of things on his mind in those days," says Dr. Halbert Fillinger. "It was a tough time for him."

Dr. Spelman was also in the process of designing a new morgue, still in use today, and eighteen months later he was thrust into the national spotlight when he worked on the autopsy of Mary Jo Kopechne, the young staffer who had drowned in Senator Edward Kennedy's car in Chappaquiddick.

Still, Dr. Molly Dapena believes, Dr. Spelman could have done more in the Marie Noe case and made a difference.

"He had it all and chose not to do anything," she now says. "To me it was amazing that we closed the book as the chief medical examiner chose not to take action."

But many feel that a weakened Spelman may have felt he no longer had the political strength to go out on a limb to rule the Noe baby deaths homicide. And even if he had done so, according to Dr. Fillinger, there was no certainty that Marie Noe would have been prosecuted.

"If the mother didn't confess there would only be

circumstantial evidence," said Fillinger in 1998. "But I know he had some suspicions because they were being voiced as the cases continued to appear."

The two doctors, who were heavy smokers, both died of lung cancer, Campbell in 1969, at just forty-four years old, and Spelman in 1971.

FOURTEEN

THE BIRTH OF SIDS

One year after the Philadelphia Police Department officially closed the Marie Noe case, a second international conference to debate crib death was held at Puget Sound in Seattle. In the six years since the first conference, the world's experts were no nearer solving the riddle of sudden infant death. This time, it was hoped, they could embark on a federally-funded, structured research program to reach their common goal.

Dr. Molly Valdez-Dapena was one of the keynote speakers at the conference, which included a distinguished group of pediatricians, pathologists, biostatisticians and immunochemists. The first order of business was to find an alternate name for crib death so coroners would have a specific condition that could be entered on the death certificate, rather than "undetermined" or "unknown," as had been the case with most of the Noe babies.

The doctors were also anxious to alleviate the guilt that many mothers felt after their babies died in unexplained circumstances, by providing a medical term to cover what was basically uncharted territory. The doctors had coined the term Sudden Death Syndrome (SDS) at their 1963 conference. Now it was decided to add an "I" for Infant to the acronym.

This was the official birth of Sudden Infant Death

Syndrome, a medically non-existent condition that would soon take on a life of its own, providing respectable cover for Marie Noe and others like her.

Molly Dapena stepped up to the podium to bring the delegates up to date with what had been accomplished in the six years since they had last met. It was in fact very little. She mentioned twelve researchers who had basically embroidered new theories on old chestnuts such as bacterial infection, nasal obstruction and electrolyte imbalances.

But in her list was one theory so outlandish and repugnant that delegates refused point-blank to even discuss it. In fact Dr. Stuart Asch had been excluded from the conference altogether, after publishing a paper suggesting that some crib deaths were in fact infanticide, as an extreme manifestation of postpartum depression.

At the time the young psychiatrist was working as a psychiatric liaison to the obstetrical department at New York's Mount Sinai Hospital. He had become interested in hostility in pregnant women and how it might find later expression with the baby. In 1968 he had published a highly controversial paper on crib death, suggesting that mothers *can* and *do* kill their babies. He believed it to be an unrecognized cause of crib deaths.

"It was very unpopular," explained Dr. Asch. "The idea that a mother will kill her baby is *so* abhorrent to western culture. People wouldn't talk to me after that."

After presenting his paper to the American Psychiatric Association, Dr. Asch became a pariah in the medical community, encountering great personal and professional difficulties. A subsequent infanticide case study, carried out with the cooperation of New York's chief medical examiner at the time, Milton Helpern, got him into even more trouble. After the *National Law Journal* published his findings that out of forty recently bereaved mothers interviewed, five were possible homicides, the Queens D.A. demanded their names with a view to prosecution.

When Dr. Asch refused to divulge the mothers' identities, saying he was a psychiatrist and not a policeman, he was threatened with jail for withholding evidence.

"I'm a physician, not a prosecuting attorney," said Dr. Asch, who then abandoned his work for four years so he wouldn't risk breaking the law.

At that time Dr. Dapena lined up with her colleagues against the maverick psychiatrist. In the audience when he had first presented the paper, Dr. Dapena had angrily risen up to challenge him, declaring that she refused to believe any mother capable of killing her child. But over the years Dr. Dapena would change her views diametrically as the evidence stacked up to support Dr. Asch.

"It was sheer ignorance, that I can attest to," said Molly Dapena in 1998. "I really can not remember my own sentiments and what they were from one time to another."

When, in an attempt to be objective, she included Dr. Asch's unpopular theory at the 1969 conference, several delegates were so angry, they sent him "hate mail."

Later in the conference Dr. Dapena was to return to the subject of infanticide, publicly stating for the first and last time Dr. Spelman's true feelings about the Marie Noe case. The now-infamous Philadelphia case was first introduced by one of the conference organizers, Dr. Abraham Bergman. He had raised the subject of whether crib death was a genetic factor that ran in families, singling out the Noe case.

"When lay persons inquire about inheritance factors, I state that at the present time there is no evidence that SIDS runs in families," Dr. Bergman declared. "They then frequently ask about the seven members of one family in Philadelphia who were alleged to die suddenly and unexpectedly. This case received a great deal of attention in the lay press: it was never reported in the scientific press."

"I am familiar with that particular family," replied Dr. Dapena, as she rose from her seat. Then, in spite of her reluctance to accept that a mother could kill her baby, she proceeded to drop a real bombshell.

"Dr. Joseph Spelman, the chief medical examiner of the city of Philadelphia, has concluded that these children did *not* die of SIDS. However, because of legal implications, we are not at liberty to report the results of his investigation."

Dapena's startling revelations were met by a complete wall of silence from the delegates, who must have been familiar with Dr. Spelman's public statement that he had no suspicions of foul play with the Noe babies.

Amazingly, not one of the delegates pursued the matter and without further questions the meeting moved on to discuss the less controversial subject of pathological anatomy.

This would be the last time Marie and Arthur Noe would be mentioned publicly in almost thirty years, as they disappeared without a trace, moving two doors down on N. American Street to make a fresh start.

Closely listening to Molly Dapena's electrifying news was Dr. Alfred Steinschneider, an ambitious thirty-nine-year-old pediatric researcher from Syracuse, New York.

It would be Steinschneider who would play a vital role in the future direction of the SIDS movement and unwittingly bring Marie Noe to justice.

At that time Steinschneider had no experience of crib death, but decided to address the delegates anyway. A highly articulate, charismatic speaker, with a doctorate in psychology, Steinschneider then offered up a theory of his own.

"We need an explanation for SIDS," he began. "There is little doubt in my mind that an abnormally intense and persistent autonomic discharge, in an otherwise normal individual, can result in sudden death."

Although he was no expert in sudden infant death, Steinschneider had specialized in the automatic reflexes that control vital body functions in babies like breathing, heartbeat and digestion functions. He was also familiar with the periodic pauses in breathing that tiny infants often experience in sleep, called *apnea*, coming from the Greek term meaning "want of breath."

Steinschneider wondered whether some babies might stop breathing altogether during an apneic episode and die. And that theory seemed just as plausible as many others then being proposed. The delegates were only too well aware that they had all been stabbing in the dark for answers. Maybe this fresh face in the SIDS crowd really had something new and valid.

"I advocate a concentrated research effort," declared Steinschneider as he finished his speech, laying the groundwork for a new career that would soon propel him to national prominence and make him a wealthy man.

Later Steinschneider would tell author Jamie Talan that he was totally out of his depth at the conference. "I felt like a novice," he admitted. "I didn't really know what I was talking about."

Nevertheless, Dr. Steinschneider returned home to Syracuse, convinced that he had a vital role to play in solving the mystery of SIDS and saving the thousands of babies who were dying every year. On his first morning back at the pediatric department at the Upstate Medical Center, he announced that he planned to devote himself full-time to SIDS. And, through the sheer force of his personality, his superiors allowed Steinschneider to close down the pediatrics clinic he was presently running and replace it with the first-ever SIDS research center.

Theorizing that some babies may be born with a defective heart or lung, predisposing them to life-threatening apneic episodes, Steinschneider decided to clinically document the breathing patterns of babies that had suffered near-miss incidents. He then appealed to pediatricians in Syracuse and beyond to alert him about any infants they encountered with any breathing problems.

In the middle of April 1970, a disheveled, sad-looking woman named Waneta Hoyt walked into the Upstate Medical Center with her one-month-old baby Molly, after being referred to Steinschneider by her pediatrician, Dr. Roger Perry. Her first three babies had all died suddenly, leaving doctors baffled. Now Waneta and her husband Tim were hoping that Dr. Steinschneider would be able to save their fourth child.

It was almost exactly what had happened to Marie Noe many years earlier.

FIFTEEN

THE CLOCK TICKS

In hindsight there were a great many similarities between Marie Noe and Waneta Hoyt. Although Waneta was eighteen years younger and raised in the rural farming community of Newark Valley in upstate New York, both women grew up in poverty with drunken, abusive fathers. They felt unloved as children and were both considered outsiders by their respective friends and families.

They would finally escape their miserable homelives and parents' tyranny by marrying weak, subservient men. Both soon became pregnant, a physical state they seemed to enjoy. The two women even resembled each other physically, with their plain, haunted looks and thinning hair.

Waneta's first baby, Eric, was born in October 1964, two months before the birth of Marie's ninth baby, Cathy. Eric Hoyt lived just three months and ten days before Waneta claimed to have found him lying on a table, limp and lifeless. She would later admit she'd murdered him, embarking on a career of serial infanticide just as Marie Noe was coming to the end of hers.

On Memorial Day 1966 Waneta gave birth to her second baby, James Avery Hoyt, and everything seemed to be fine as he grew up into a strong, healthy little boy. Two years later Waneta became pregnant for the third time, giving birth to Julie Marie on July 17, 1968. By this time Little Arty was already six months dead and the Philadelphia police had stopped investigating the Noes.

By September 5, Julie was dead, her mother tearfully explaining that she had been feeding her cereal when she suddenly began to choke and went limp. Three weeks later Waneta staggered out of her house carrying James' dead body to a neighbors'.

"I was getting dressed," she sobbed. "He came to me, he just collapsed in my arms."

As in the Noe case, doctors and pathologists were dumbfounded by the untimely deaths of Waneta's three children, believing them to have been caused by a hereditary factor they knew nothing about. Others wondered . . .

When Waneta gave birth to a healthy baby girl, Molly, in mid-March 1970, there was little cause for celebration. Two weeks later Waneta called the rescue squad in a panic; they arrived at her house to find little Molly still breathing but turning blue. It was a near-miss and her concerned pediatrician Dr. Roger Perry subjected the baby to three days of strenuous tests, which all came back negative.

As a last resort he suggested Waneta and Molly drive the seventy miles to Syracuse to see Dr. Steinschneider, who had launched his new SIDS research unit a year earlier. Steinschneider immediately decided that Molly was the perfect case study to prove his apnea theory and immediately admitted the baby for an indefinite period, so he could personally test her. Baby Molly was wired up twenty-four hours a day to an apnea monitor, which sounded an alarm if there were any irregularities in breathing.

On May 8, Steinschneider finally discharged Molly back to her parents, convinced that she had suffered numerous instances of apnea. Other doctors would consider that these fifteen-second lapses were normal but Steinschneider believed he was onto something vitally important, a possible key to unlock the SIDS mystery.

Molly was sent home with her own portable apnea monitor and her mother was briefed on how to use it. Within days the baby was back in the SIDS unit after Waneta reported that the machine's alarm had been going off periodically. The baby remained there for weeks, and just like little Cathy Noe five years earlier, Steinschneider's nurses began to suspect, as the nuns at St. Joseph's had with Marie Noe, that it might not be a medical problem at all. The nurses noticed that Waneta Hoyt seemed totally apathetic to her baby and even uncomfortable with her.

Molly came home after nine days in the unit but the following morning Waneta reported that she had suffered two apneic attacks during the first night. Steinschneider was highly sympathetic, immediately re-admitting Molly for further tests, which lasted ten days. She was then discharged for the last time.

The next morning Molly was dead. Waneta explained that she had found her baby turning blue and not breathing. An autopsy was performed and the cause of death registered as "interstitial pneumonitis."

Two months later Waneta telephoned Steinschneider to say that she was once again pregnant. He was delighted at the news. Now he would have another baby from the same family to study. He immediately instructed her to bring it to him straight from maternity after it was born.

And that is exactly what happened when Noah Timothy Hoyt was four days old on May 13, 1971. This time the testing was even more exhaustive than it had been for Molly. Although Dr. Steinschneider was observing many other babies in his unit, Noah was singled out for special treatment.

After a month of observation, Noah finally went home for the first time and was hooked up to a home apnea monitor. But the next day he was in the emergency room after Waneta claimed he had stopped breathing and she had revived him using mouth-to-mouth resuscitation. Convinced that the baby had survived a near-miss, Steinschneider readmitted him to continue his tests.

Five weeks later Noah returned home, to the alarm of his nurses who believed him to be in grave danger. When they confided their fears to Steinschneider, he assured them there was nothing to worry about. But within twenty-four hours little Noah was back in the SIDS unit, after his mother complained that he had started to cough and then turned different colors during a feeding. He left again the same evening for what would be the final time.

By the next morning Noah was dead in his crib, still attached to his apnea monitor. A tearful Waneta later told Steinschneider that she had walked in to find her baby turning blue and not breathing. An autopsy was carried out and the immediate cause of death listed as "acute Bronchiolitis."

Steinschneider was now convinced that the Hoyt babies proved his theory and that SIDS was a genetic condition which runs in families.

*   *   *

Dr. Alfred Steinschneider published his landmark paper on SIDS in the October 1972 issue of *Pediatrics*. The crucial findings, which connected SIDS with prolonged periods of Apnea, were his case studies of the two Hoyt babies, referred to as M.H. and N.H.

Entitled "Prolonged Apnea and the Sudden Infant Death Syndrome: Clinical and Laboratory Observations," the paper had a profound effect on the medical community. One of the major points it made, borne out by his detailed studies of the two Hoyt babies, was that SIDS was genetic.

"I think what basically happened in 1972," said Dallas-based forensic pathologist Linda Norton, who would be instrumental in helping to bring Waneta Hoyt to justice a quarter of a century later, "is that the pediatric community at large accepted Steinschneider's notion that this is something that runs in families. Then we began to get medical validation for women who were murdering their children. And not just medical validation. These women were being comforted and rewarded for murdering their children."

Over the next few years millions of federal dollars would be channeled into SIDS research as it took on the trappings of a crusade with Steinschneider at the helm. In 1974 President Richard Nixon signed the Sudden Infant Death Syndrome Act into law, signifying a national commitment to provide funds for research and counseling for parents.

"You're dealing with a political movement in the 1970s with regards to SIDS," said Dr. Norton. "People seemed to lose all reason and rationality."

*　　*　　*

Arthur and Marie Noe must have been delighted to read the various newspaper reports of the SIDS breakthrough. In fact Marie had been invited to address a SIDS meeting, but had refused, saying that it would be too emotional an experience. The Noes now viewed themselves as pioneers, finally vindicated after years of finger-pointing and suspicion. Marie even carried around SIDS newspaper articles to show friends and family, until they eventually turned yellow with overuse.

In 1977 a British pediatrician named Dr. Roy Meadow identified a new diagnosis, Munchausen's syndrome by proxy, to explain why mothers murdered their children. Named after the legendary eighteenth-century compulsive liar Baron Karl von Munchausen, it entered medical literature when Dr. Meadow published his findings in the prestigious medical publication, *The Lancet*.

Dr. Meadow's theory was that these mothers suffered from a variant of Munchausen's Syndrome, a bizarre mental condition where people feign or induce illness in order to get care or nurturing from doctors. In Munchausen's-By-Proxy, people instead injure their children to gain attention and sympathy. The children become the tools through which they weaved increasingly complex relationships with their doctors and nurses and nurturance from family, friends or the community.

Usually Munchausen mothers will suffocate or poison their babies, and then sound the alarm when they are on the brink of death. Often they go too far and accidentally commit murder.

"These sympathy junkies," said Dr. Vincent Di Maio, medical examiner of San Antonio, Texas, "usually keep killing until they're caught or they run out of children."

English forensic pathologist Professor Christopher Gardess calls these women the quiet, clandestine serial killers that our society is loath to recognize.

"It's a cat and mouse game," he explained. "The intention is never to kill or permanently harm. It's a risk game, a dicing with danger and then putting it right."

But Dr. Stuart Asch, who has studied both the Noe and Hoyt cases, believes that the forces that drive them to murder may be far more complex than Munchausen's Syndrome-By-Proxy.

"There's many things involved in infanticide," he explained. "Marie appears to be doing this to get attention directed to herself and I don't think it's Munchausen's. The serial infanticides are all self-involved. The babies mean nothing. Marie was reveling in the attention people paid to her. She became alive when the baby was dead because of all the attention."

Dr. Halbert Fillinger, who would be called by the D.A. to testify in the Noe case as an expert witness, believes Marie Noe's case may be so uncommon as to defy psychological labeling.

"She's a strange lady," said Fillinger, who has made a study of psychological profiling. "A homicide detective told me how he was unable to understand her thought processes, as she seemed totally unaffected by losing all her children. They had never seen any guilty person whose mind worked like hers."

Although one possible motive may have been insurance, Dr. Fillinger believes it to be far simpler. "Marie didn't seem to want children, despite the fact that she bore them," he explained. "I think that the idea was not just to have sex, the idea was to have a baby. And then after the baby came it was not wanted. And whether or not it was because that baby wasn't perfect, or that baby cried, or for whatever reason, she grew hostile. It's been suggested that Arthur wanted children and so she gave him babies. Then she changed her mind."

Without doubt Arthur Noe remains one of the greatest mysteries of the case. Constantly standing by his wife and never questioning her involvement, the small, feisty, well-intentioned Arthur always viewed his children's deaths as acts of God.

"I often wondered what he was thinking every time a baby died," said Dr. Fillinger. "He loves kids, or says he does, and then every time they have a kid, it's lost."

SIXTEEN

JUST REWARDS

Jimmy Carter was elected thirty-ninth President of the United States on November 2, 1976, and it proved the kiss of death for Kensington. During his campaign Carter had promised southern voters thousands of new jobs by relocating northern textile mills and factories. And within a couple of years of his election, Kensington went into freefall as factory owners accepted generous federal tax subsidies to move South, causing massive unemployment. After a century and a half, Kensington's once-thriving textile industry ground to a halt and disappeared, leaving scores of abandoned factories and burned-out buildings in its wake.

"They were supposed to take the factory workers out of here and relocate them," said Joe McGovern, who lost his job when the factories closed. "They never did."

Kensington was falling apart at the seams and its population, which had already plummeted from one hundred and fifty-five thousand in 1920 to less than one hundred thousand in 1960, now sank even lower. And as the white workers abandoned ship, they were replaced by a new wave of black and Hispanic immigrants, causing much resentment in the neighborhood.

Elderly Kensingtonians on the poverty line, like Arthur and Marie Noe—who stopped going to St. Hugh's Church when the mass went Spanish for the new, predominantly Hispanic, congregation—could not afford to move out to the smarter suburbs around Philadelphia. They watched with trepidation as their neighborhood—now known as "the Badlands"—deteriorated into a crime-ridden no-man's-land, where it was no longer safe to walk the streets because of the violence and drugs.

"It's a war zone out there," explained local city activist Regina Farrell. "The good people of Kensington hid out in their houses because they were fearful."

By the mid-80s the gangs moved in, seeing a ripe opportunity to exploit the run-down neighborhood for huge profits. They had no trouble recruiting the legions of unemployed teenagers, who had few prospects and were looking for easy money, and before long Kensington had established itself as the hard drugs center of Philadelphia.

"The drugs come across the river from Camden, New Jersey," said Farrell, who would later lead a local fight against drugs in the 1990s with Operation Sunrise.

In a highly organized operation the drug barons shipped narcotics in from Jamaica, the Dominican Republic and Florida. Drug activity flourished on four corners in the neighborhood, where dealers wore different-colored baseball caps to signify their drug for sale.

After his factory closed Arthur Noe used his connections as a local Democratic committeeman to find a number of minor jobs with the city. He served as an aide to his ward leader and hero, Harry Jannotti, until the councilman's fall from grace in the 1979 Abscam sting, and he then found a clerical job with the Philadelphia Gas Works until he retired in 1986.

Marie also benefited from Arthur's political friends

with a job in the Philadelphia Traffic Court from 1977 to 1984, and then one in the Philadelphia Parking Authority Garage. In 1990, after a three-month stint as a clerk in a state legislator's office, she retired at the age of sixty-two.

By the mid-1990s the Noes had receded into respectable old age and anonymity, the untimely deaths of their ten children just dimly remembered local folklore.

On March 24, 1994, a time-bomb began ticking under the Noes when Waneta Hoyt confessed to suffocating her five children. Justice had finally caught up with the balding forty-seven-year-old housewife after a tenacious assistant prosecutor in upstate New York read Dr. Steinschneider's 1972 SIDS manifesto while investigating a baby who had been killed by its father.

He immediately suspected that the two unnamed babies from one family, who played such a pivotal role in Steinschneider's acclaimed theory, had been murdered. But after identifying them as Molly and Noah Hoyt, it would take years to persuade the local district attorney to prosecute.

Although Waneta retracted her confession before her murder trial, she was found guilty and sentenced to fifteen years to life on each of the five charges. As the judge ordered terms to be served consecutively, Waneta Hoyt faced a minimum of seventy-five years in jail, where she would die in 1999.

The conviction immediately brought Dr. Steinschneider's theory that SIDS runs in families into question. The doctor, who had now moved to Atlanta where he had become president of the American SIDS Institute, stood by his findings, refusing to admit that they were flawed. But many law enforcement officers and medical experts now believed that all parents who had lost two or more children to SIDS should be investigated as possible murder suspects.

Dr. Linda Norton, who testified in the Hoyt case and was instrumental in bringing it to trial, believes this is the tip of the iceberg and that the number of murdered babies could run into the thousands. "I hate to think about it," she says. "I hope the medical profession will come back to its senses."

On the day of Waneta Hoyt's arrest, a journalist for *Newsday* named Richard Firstman heard the news on National Public Radio and was intrigued. Realizing its larger implications for destroying the credibility of Steinschneider's SIDS theory, he decided to investigate further and was joined by his wife Jamie Talan, who was a science editor at *Newsday*.

"My husband had been looking to write a book," explained Talan. "He came over to my desk and said, 'I think we have one.' "

Talan immediately went to work researching Waneta Hoyt and everything she could read on SIDS. There, buried away in the medical literature, she came across Dr. Molly Dapena's two brief mentions of Marie Noe's dead children at the 1963 and 1969 SIDS conferences.

"I just couldn't believe that this couple could have ten dead kids and have gotten away with murder," said Talan. "I became obsessed with the case and discovered they were still alive and living in Philadelphia."

By this time Firstman and Talen had signed a book deal, for what was to become *The Death of Innocents*. Talan decided to try and resurrect the Noes' case and bring them to justice, but when she called Philadelphia

District Attorney Lynne Abraham's office, she was met with a wall of silence. Abraham refused to take her calls and nobody in the D.A.'s office seemed at all interested in hearing any new information that might shed light on the case after so many years.

She then put in a call to the now-retired chief of homicide to try to get him interested.

"He laughed at me," said Talan. "He said, 'Why are you calling me? Don't you think we have enough cases already?' It seemed to me that society was saying, 'We don't care if you kill your kids!' "

Talan, a mother herself who even had nightmares about the dead babies, then played detective, tracking down the Noes' unlisted telephone number. She called them up and spent an hour talking to Arthur and Marie about their children. She even planned to visit them in Kensington, but Firstman stopped her, warning that they would only play a minor role in their book.

Eventually when the six-hundred-thirty-two–page book was published to critical acclaim in early 1997, it had six brief mentions of the Noes under the "Moore" pseudonym which *Life* had used in 1963. "The 'Moores' never left Philadelphia," it said at the end, enigmatically. "They can be found living out their lives there. They have no grandchildren." Firstman and Talan had deliberately planted the vital clue that would ultimately lead to the arrest and downfall of Marie Noe.

When a senior reporter at *Philadelphia* Magazine named Stephen Fried happened to read the book, he immediately spotted the reference to the Noes and was assigned to the story by his editor. Now the clock for Marie Noe was ticking louder than ever.

*   *   *

By Fall 1997—twenty-nine years after the death of Little Arty—most of the protagonists in the case were either dead or retired. Dr. Spelman had died in 1971 and Marie Noe's long-suffering family practitioner Dr. Gangemi eleven years later. But OME investigator Joe McGillen was still alive and considered the Noes unfinished business.

Now in his seventies, the once-relentless sleuth, who believed his years of work had been torpedoed by Joseph Schimpf, often thought about Marie Noe, but had long given up hope that she would ever be brought to justice. In 1984 he had left the medical examiner's office and moved out of Philadelphia with his wife Elaine, seeking a quieter life away from the daily horror of investigating the dead. "I'm just an ordinary guy in retirement," he says modestly today.

Although the police and the medical examiner's office had destroyed all the case files, McGillen still had his own set carefully packed away in his garage. These would prove crucial ammunition for finally bringing Marie Noe to justice.

Philadelphia Homicide Detective Sergeant Larry Nodiff, who was in charge of unsolved cases in the special investigations unit, was also intrigued about the Noes.

The six-foot, immaculately groomed detective was told about the references to the Noes in *The Death Of Innocents* by Stephen Fried and had quietly reactivated the case, as there was no statute of limitations on serial murder. Ironically, had the first four Noe babies survived, they would have been older than he was.

The McGillen reports were a treasure trove of intimate details about the strange lives of Arthur and Marie Noe, painstakingly culled from friends and family. There were medical reports on the babies as well as highly revealing information from doctors and nurses, who had been suspicious about the babies' deaths.

Detective Nodiff's predecessor in the homicide department, Schimpf, still saw no reason to reopen the case, adamantly standing by his report, which exonerated Marie. Now in his late seventies, the once-robust detective has undergone two quadruple bypass operations and was chronically ill with Parkinson's.

"She's a little bit wifty, you know," he rasped over the phone, when asked about Marie Noe. "You'd have to see her, I guess, to figure her out. There didn't appear to be anything wrong to me."

In late 1997, Sergeant Nodiff called a summit meeting to discuss the Marie Noe case and see if he should proceed further and go to the district attorney's office. In attendance were Dr. Molly Dapena, Dr. Halbert Fillinger, Joe McGillen and *Philadelphia* Magazine reporter Stephen Fried, who had started interviewing Arthur and Marie Noe and gained their trust.

The two pathologists, who had both autopsied several of the Noe babies, had not seen each other in three decades. Molly Dapena was now an active seventy-eight-year-old, whose memory wasn't what it used to be. The one-time SIDS ingenue was now its respected doyenne.

Fillinger, too, was no longer the young forensic pathologist he had been when he was first called into the case. Now the respected coroner of Montgomery County, the white-haired seventy-two-year-old was still recovering from a recent car accident outside his office. But his injuries had not in the least dampened his wry sense of humor; his jokey business cards listed his various occupations as "Fly Swatters – Racing Forms –

Autopsies Performed – Used Cars – Whiskey – Manure – Nails – Land," and his car bore the personalized plate, "Homicide Hal."

Now, sitting around a conference table at the *Philadelphia* magazine offices on Market Street, the two doctors and Joe McGillen cast their minds back over the years to one of the biggest cases of their careers.

"It was amazing to me, because we closed the book," said Dr. Dapena, who was seeing the reports together for the first time. "All this information had been given to the chief medical examiner, Dr. Spelman, but he chose not to take action."

As Nodiff and his team of experts, now in retirement, carefully studied the numerous reports in front of them, each felt a growing excitement that they might be able to solve the case at last. Finally, they would get to see all the pieces of the puzzle, instead of just the few they had been involved with.

By the end of the meeting everyone agreed that there wasn't the slightest doubt that Marie Noe had systematically killed her children. Finally, Molly Dapena was sure of Marie Noe's guilt, declaring her disbelief that she is still "as free as a bird."

"Now it's as clear as day," she would say later. "I think the woman is demented. This woman is not with us and never was."

Dr. Fillinger said his whole concept of the case changed on reading all the damning evidence together.

"This file really accuses them of murder," he told Sergeant Nodiff, who would later receive a commendation for his work in the Noe investigation. "I would have to go to the D.A. and say these people should be investigated."

As they left police headquarters, everyone at the meeting agreed that there was still a serial murderer on the loose in Philadelphia, who must be brought to justice. But the real problem would be persuading Philadelphia D.A. Lynne Abraham and the chief of her homicide unit, Charles Gallagher, to take up the case and prosecute.

The years had not been kind to Marie and Arthur Noe, who had both been wracked by illness. Anyone seeing them on their frequent walks along the boardwalk at Atlantic City might have mistaken them for any other elderly couple trying their luck in the casinos. There was nothing on the surface to make the casual observer even give them a second look.

Now almost seventy, Marie's once-blonde hair, which Arthur had so admired half a century earlier, was dirty gray and coming out by the handful. Washed-out eyes hid furtively in a ghostlike marmoreal face, which seemed devoid of all expression. Her once-robust frame had been stiffened by rheumatoid arthritis and a right knee replacement three years earlier. She was also diabetic and had recently undergone a gall bladder operation.

Marie's father, James Lyddy, had died of cancer in 1974 at the age of eighty-three, and her mother, Ella, had passed on two years later at the age of eighty-five. Arthur Noe, now seventy-seven years old and recovering from a stroke, had stubbornly refused to obey his doctors and continued to chain-smoke. Riddled by arthritis, bloodshot eyes and a bulbous drinker's nose dominated his cavernous face, giving him a haunted look. Although he seemed spent and lonely, his combativeness remained, as Stephen Fried found out when he began regular visits to N. American Street in the fall of 1997. "I thought you were a writer?" Arthur once told Fried, after challenging him with the word "philoprogenitiveness" in an impromptu game of one-upmanship. Ironically, the man who saw so many of his children die at the hands of his wife was referring to a word meaning "motherly love."

Over the last thirty years, the Noes had turned the new house they'd moved into after Little Arty's death into a shrine to their dead children. Joyful color pictures of Cathy at the beach line the walls and there are framed pictures of many of the other babies arranged around the living room. Now in their old age, they both knew it was only a matter of time before they would join them.

"People are gonna think what they think," snapped Marie defensively when Fried broached the subject of the renewed interest in babies who had died of SIDS. "I know I often question myself about each of them babies . . . you feel it's your fault, and you coulda [sic] prevented it . . ."

"You're not responsible, Marie," interjected her husband. "It's just something that happened."

In mid-January 1998, for the first time in three decades, the Noes were front-page news again when the *Philadelphia Daily News* got wind of Fried's investigation and broke the story. Under the headline: "EIGHT TOTS: SIDS OR SERIAL KILLINGS?—Parents Say They've Nothing to Hide," veteran crime reporter Ron Avery exclusively reported that the Noe case had been reopened after lying dormant for so many years. He quoted Dapena and Fillinger, both publicly calling for a new investigation.

"We were suspicious but we couldn't prove anything," Dr. Fillinger told the *Daily News*. "When you get one SIDS death in the family, that's tragic, so you watch the second child very closely. If there's a third death, that's the time for an intense criminal investigation."

Dr. Dapena, who now claimed that she had protested to Dr. Spelman about the once-common practice of giving "pneumonia" as the cause of infant death if nothing else could be found, was even more outspoken.

"When you get four, five, six deaths in the same family, that's not SIDS. Most likely, that's infanticide."

When Ron Avery visited the Noe's house he found them eager to defend themselves, complaining that reopening the case would only bring them more misery.

"We've been through hell," Arthur Noe told Avery during an extensive two-hour interview. "Why bring back a lot of bad memories?"

They had initially refused the interview, but Arthur and Marie's love of publicity got the better of them and they invited Avery into their living room to talk.

"The last thing I want to see is this thing brought up again," said Arthur between puffs on a cigarette. "It brings up all the pain and troubles and heartaches. Maybe it's news to others, but it's pain to us."

Well aware that homicide detectives were back on their trail after the debunking of Dr. Steinschneider's SIDS theory, Arthur borrowed President Franklin Roosevelt's famous quote, saying that he and Marie had nothing to fear but fear itself.

Avery was surprised by the completely emotionless

way in which Marie talked about her dead children. She told him that although she couldn't stop the case being reopened, she was concerned about her babies' bodies being exhumed, saying: "I just don't want them disturbed."

According to Marie, she thought about her babies "all the time" and even wondered if she had been an "overprotective" mother, saying that she always did something wrong.

"Now they tell you to keep a child on [its] back," she said. "One of our children died on her back. There is no answer."

Asked why they kept having baby after baby, Arthur said their Catholic priest kept urging them to have children. In those days, he confided to Avery, they didn't believe in birth control.

"There's no harm in wanting a baby," he said, anxiously wringing his hands. "All I wanted was one child, and if we had more, that would have been all right."

Telling Avery that they were desperate to move from their block because of the constant drug-dealing and violence, Arthur contemplated the one good thing he could see in his ten children's deaths.

"The only thing I am thankful for," he rasped in his smoker's voice, "is that they never got to use drugs or got sent to Vietnam. That was a hell hole."

SEVENTEEN

DON'T TELL MY HUSBAND

The clock finally stopped ticking for Marie Noe at 4:30 p.m. on Wednesday, March 15, 1998, when a police car drew up in front of her N. American Street home. Homicide detectives had been working the Noe case for almost six months, but were forced to act after Stephen Fried's damning article had been published in *Philadelphia* Magazine the day before.

With the banner headline, "Ten Dead Babies: Medical Mystery . . . or Murder?" the twelve-thousand-word cover story was a powerful indictment of Marie Noe and pulled no punches. Fried's editors were so concerned about the controversial story that they printed two separate covers; the Noe article on the covers of mailed-out subscription copies, and a less-contentious study of city real estate for the newsstands.

The article threw down the gauntlet for the police, speculating that any day a homicide detective would come knocking at the Noes' door and make an arrest. "If he arrives before death does, they will have some explaining to do," it concluded.

It was in fact three homicide detectives who arrived at the Noes'. Detectives John McDermott and Steven Vivarina from the Special Investigations Unit remained in the car while Sergeant Larry Nodiff rang the bell. Arthur and Marie were finishing an early dinner. When they answered, Nodiff asked them to accompany him downtown for questioning about their babies' deaths. The detective told them that they weren't being arrested and could refuse, but Arthur agreed to cooperate. Then, turning to Marie he said: "Will you put Asshole downstairs?"

When Nodiff looked mystified by the remark, Arthur explained that Asshole was the name of one of their pet cats. Another was called "Mommy."

At 6:00 p.m. the Noes arrived at police headquarters, recently rebuilt and named after the original Roundhouse, which dominates Franklin Square on the corner of Race and 8th Street. They were immediately brought up to Room 104 on the second floor, which serves as the Homicide Department. There they were split up and sent to separate interrogation rooms: Marie was in Room D with Detective Vivarina, and Arthur in the adjoining Room C with Detective McDermott. Sergeant Nodiff remained outside to observe the interrogations through a hidden closed-circuit camera, which had only been installed a few days earlier.

McDermott got little out of Arthur Noe, who remained steadfastly loyal to Marie. After a couple of hours he was allowed out and not even asked to make a formal statement. The detective offered to drive him home but he insisted on waiting outside for his wife. Then he sat through the night chain-smoking and watching television as Marie faced her interrogators.

The cramped, off-white interrogation room measured just ten feet by six feet and was in need of a new coat of paint. In the corner sat an old wooden chair with a pair of handcuffs dangling from it and there was a small square two-way mirror to the left of the front door.

Although the surroundings might be daunting, Detective Vivarina's manner certainly was not. The amiable detective was known in the department for using his warm personality to connect with suspects and loosen their tongues. And it was Sergeant Vivarina who would finally succeed where so many detectives had failed over the last fifty years.

By 11:30 p.m. Marie Noe had given up the terrible secrets she had kept buried for so long. She had finally come out and admitted killing her children and agreed to make a full confession. She was then read her rights by Vivarina as McDermott set up a recording device and Sergeant Nodiff sat in as a witness.

Marie seemed strangely calm as she was told that she had the right to remain silent and anything she said could be used against her. She was also told that she could consult a lawyer before she made her statement, but declined the offer. By each of the seven Miranda questions read to her off the official police form, she scrawled her initials.

At 12:05 a.m. on Thursday morning Marie Noe took a deep breath, composed herself and began a dramatic confession that would end more than half-a-century of lies about her children. Even the hardened detectives would be amazed at the total lack of emotion in her voice as she detailed her monstrous actions as if they were commonplace. It seemed as though she was talking about somebody else.

Q: Mrs. Noe, my name is Detective John McDermott #9005, and with us is Detective Steve Vivarina #900, and we are from the Homicide Division. Do you understand that we are investigating the deaths of your children, specifically Richard Allen Noe on 4/7/49, Elizabeth Mary Noe on 2/17/51, Jacqueline Noe on 5/14/52, Arthur Noe, Jr., on 5/6/55, Constance Noe on 3/24/58, Mary Lee Noe on 1/4/63, Catherine Ellen Noe on 2/25/66, and Arthur Joseph Noe on 1/2/68.

A: Yes, I understand.

Q: Have you understood your rights as they have been explained to you?

A: Yeah, I've been Mirandized before down here, back after the last child passed away, that was Arthur Joseph Noe. They gave me a polygraph test then too.

Q: Are you presently under the influence of either drugs or alcohol?

A: No.

Q: Are you under medication for any condition for medical treatment?

A: Just for diabetes, that's all, pills, not the needle.

Q: Marie, have you ever been treated for a mental condition?

A: No, I haven't.

Q: What was the last grade you completed in school?

A: Fifth grade.

Q: Can you read, write and understand English?

A: Yeah, now I do, I've learned since I've been married, my husband has helped me a lot.

Q: Marie, we are going to ask you to recall the circumstances of each of your children's death, beginning with the first death, that of Richard Allen Noe on 4/7/49. Is this all right with you?

A: Yeah. I'll start at the beginning. Richard was born on March 7, 1949, and he was very sickly after he came home from the hospital, he was throwing up and he had loose bowels. At first I thought that it might have been colic, and my sister, Frances, thought that it was colic too. She came around to see what she could do to help, and she told me that if I kept his belly warm, it might help.

After the ten [10] days' stay in the hospital, at Temple Hospital, Richard came home with me. When he kept throwing up, I took him back to Temple Hospital, but they wouldn't keep him, they didn't know what to do for him, and I took him back home. The next couple of days, he was still sick, and then I took him down to St. Christopher's Hospital, at 4th and Lehigh Ave. The doctors examined him and decided to keep him, and he was there for about two [2] weeks.

He was only home for a few days, maybe five [5] or so, and he was always crying. He couldn't tell me what was bothering him, he just kept crying.

The day that he died, I bathed him and put him in nightclothes, and I was going to put him down for the night. I put him on his belly instead of his back in his bassinet, and there was a pillow under his face, he was lying face down. Then I took my hand and pressed his face down into the pillow until he stopped moving. After this, I went and layed [sic] down and a couple of hours later, my husband Art came home from work, he was working the 3 p.m. until 12 a.m. shift. When Art came home, he found Richard in the bassinet. Art wanted to hold Richard, and he picked him up and found that he was cold. He told me that there was something wrong with Richard, and I told Art that he was sound asleep a minute ago, but I knew that wasn't true. We wrapped him up and went to Episcopal Hospital, and they did what they could, but they could not revive him. They came out and told us that he was dead on arrival.

Q: Marie, is there anything else that you can recall with regard to Richard's death?

A: No, that's about it.

Q: Marie, with regard to the death of Elizabeth Noe, what can you tell us?

A: She was born on September 8, 1950, and I was taking her to a pediatrician at 'J' & Eric Avenue, because my husband had Blue Cross back then. Elizabeth was born healthy, and she was pretty good until she got a cold, then she got cranky. I was working then, too, at a ribbon factory at 8th & Allegheny Avenue, and my sister-in-law would watch Elizabeth while I was working. It was a little too much on me, between working full-time and taking care of the baby, so I quit the job to stay here and take care of her.

When Elizabeth caught a cold, she ended up with a high fever, about 105 degrees, so I took her to Dr. Schaeffer, and she got better. About two or three weeks after this is when she died. She was in the bassinet, I put her on her back, and then I took a pillow from the bed and put the pillow over her face and suffocated her. She was fussing, Elizabeth was a lot stronger than Richard was, and she was fighting when the pillow was over her face. I held the pillow over her face until she stopped moving.

After that I layed [sic] down on the sofa, and about half an hour or an hour later, my brother-in-law, Charles Noe, came over. He found her in the bassinet, and he said that something was wrong. I went over and put my hand on her, and she felt cold. I told Charles to call the police, and they came in no time at all. The rescue squad came too, and they told me that she was dead, but that they had to take her to the hospital to make it legal, they took her to Episcopal, I believe, but I'm not positive about that.

Q: Marie, do you recall what happened after Elizabeth died?

A: Well, after this happened, we moved out of my mother-in-law's house, that was at 240 West Atlantic Street. After Elizabeth died we moved to 215 West Ontario Street, an apartment, it was three rooms.

I got pregnant again, and Jacqueline was born, It was about two years later. She was born at Episcopal Hospital, I went through the clinic there, so

I had to see any doctor who was on duty, not one regular doctor. After I delivered the baby, I signed out of the hospital early, after about five [5] days, because my husband Art was sick at home. Jacqueline stayed in the hospital for the full ten [10] days until she came home.

Q: How long was Jacqueline home before she died?

A: Not too long, about three [3] weeks, if that.

Q: What can you tell us about the circumstances surrounding Jacqueline's death?

A: I really can't remember how Jacqueline died. All I remember about that day is that I found her lying on the bed, and she was blue and not breathing. I grabbed a blanket and went running to my mother's house at 229 West Tioga Street, about a block away. When I got to my mother's, my sister Frances was there, and she went with me to Episcopal Hospital. I was hoping that Jacqueline was alive, but after she was taken into the hospital, they came out and told me that she died.

My sister Frances was still there with me when I found out, another lady who was with us, Mrs. Schwem, had already left, she owned a grocery store and had to go back to it. I remember that the detectives came to the hospital and asked me questions about what had happened. I told them that I found the child turning blue on the bed and I grabbed a blanket and went flying to my mother's house. That was about it, the detectives never came out to the apartment or anything.

Q: Do you remember how Jacqueline died?

A: No, I can't remember if I suffocated her or she was just choking, I just remember finding her and taking her to the hospital.

Q: Marie, who was the next child born?

A: That would be Arthur, he was the second boy.

Q: What can you recall about Arthur Jr.?

A: He was only with us for a short time, he was born at either Episcopal or St. Luke's Hospital. We were living at 3452 North Rosehill Street then, I think it was in 1955. He resembled my husband's brother, he had long dark hair, it looked like it was going to be curly.

   I remember that I went to a private ambulance company that was on Tioga Street at either 'A' or 'B' Street, and I asked the man there if I had a problem with my child, would he come and take him to the hospital. The man told me that I would have to pay $200.00 to join or that he couldn't help me, so I didn't join.

Q: Why would you inquire about a private ambulance company responding to your home?

A: Because I was worried about what happened with the other three babies, that if the street was blocked I wouldn't be able to get Arthur to the hospital if something happened to him.

Q: Did you plan on harming Arthur?

A: No, but I didn't plan on harming any of the children.

Q: Do you remember the day that Arthur Jr. died?

A: I only remember bits and pieces about Arthur dying. I can remember calling for the rescue squad, but I don't remember if I did anything to Arthur or not. I remember that we went to Episcopal Hospital and I was there by myself, and I found out that he was dead.

Q: Do you recall how or where Arthur died in your home that day?

A: No.

Q: Did Arthur ever receive treatment at a hospital or a medical facility prior to the day he died?

A: I don't remember if he did or not.

Q: Marie, do you know who the next child would be?

A: Yes, Constance. We had moved to 3447 N. American Street when she was born, and I was working at Arrow Designs, on Glenwood Avenue. I took a leave of absence when I was six months pregnant because they didn't want me to get hurt at work. She was born at St. Luke's Hospital, an old doctor friend of my mother's was taking care of me at the hospital, Dr. Shartook. I don't remember the date that Connie was born, but it was in 1958, I think.

Q: What can you tell us about Constance's death?

A: She was only home for a month or a month and a half, and the day it happened, I remember what I did. She was on a chair in the parlor, and I put a pillow behind her on the chair and another chair in front so in case she rolled, she wouldn't get hurt.

I was trying to train her how to sit up in the chair. I don't know why, but I took a pillow and laid her down on the chair, and I suffocated her.

Then I went upstairs to the bathroom, and I heard the front door open while I was up there. It was my husband Arthur coming in. He had been out. When Arthur came in, I was still up in the bathroom. Arthur went out and got one of the neighbors, Mrs. Zimba, and he brought her in. I came downstairs from the bathroom, and she was trying to do CPR on Connie. Art was afraid to do it, because he didn't want to hurt the child. Either Art or I called 911, and the rescue squad came fast. They took Connie to Episcopal Hospital, and they worked on her in the back. They called the detectives, and the people from the hospital told us to sit and wait for the detectives, so we did. When the detectives got there, they asked us an awful lot of questions, and they even came back to our house and looked around.

I believe that one of the coroners even came out to the house that time, and he asked Arthur and I questions. He took a bottle of milk and a bottle of water with Karo in it to test it. We didn't even have Connie buried yet, and the detectives came out to the house again to ask more questions.

Q: Were you concerned that the police would find out that you killed Constance?

A: I was hoping that they would. I knew what I was doing was very wrong.

Q: Did the police lead you to believe that they suspected you in causing the death of either Constance or any of your other children at that time?

A: No, not really. Not until the last children died, that would be Catherine and Arthur Joseph, did I think that the police suspected me. They were stricter after the last two children died, before that, they were very nice to us.

Q: Marie, after Constance died, who was the next child?

A: Letitia was born after Connie, but she was stillborn, she never left the hospital, St. Luke's.

Q: Which child was born after Letitia?

A: It was Mary Lee, she was my first c-section. She was born in 1962 at St. Joe's [sic] Hospital. She was the first baby who was being treated by Dr. Gangemi, my last three children were being treated by him. He was a good doctor.

Q: What can you tell us about the day that Mary Lee died?

A: Not much. I can't recall that day.

Q: Who was the next child after Mary Lee Noe?

A: Terry, she was born alive, but she died in the hospital, at St. Joe's [sic] Hospital.

Q: After Terry, which baby was born next?

A: It was Catherine, she was born in December, it was either 1963 or 1964. She was born at St. Joseph's, the doctor insisted that she stay in the hospital for a while after she was born so I could recuperate from my surgery and give them a chance to do tests on her. Catherine was in the hospital for about six months until she was allowed to come home.

She was in good health after she came home from the hospital. All I can remember about the day she died was that I had her in the playpen, and I heard her fall down. She was very blue when I got to her. I got on the phone right away and dialed 911, and a policeman was there almost immediately. The policeman told me to do CPR, and then he tried it, but it wasn't working at all. She died at Episcopal Hospital, too.

Q: Marie, do you recall if you harmed Catherine in any way?

A: No, I can't remember if I did anything to her or not.

Q: Do you recall Catherine ever going back to the hospital before her death?

A: Yeah, twice that I recall. Once for a fever, and another time because she wasn't breathing right.

Q: How old was Catherine when she died?

A: She was fourteen months old, she was the child that lived the longest. After she died, we had the coroner and detectives again at the house, they were asking questions again. They took bottles again, and samples of food that she ate that day. One of the detectives even checked around the house to see if we had a gas leak, but at that time we had a pet bird, and it was living, so they knew that we didn't have a leak.

Q: Marie, what was the name of the next child who was born?

A: Arthur Joseph, he was my last child.

Q: How old was Arthur Joseph when he died?

A: He wasn't very old, he was three or four months old. He was in and out of the hospital a couple of times because he had trouble breathing.

Q: What can you tell us about Arthur Joseph's death?

A: No, I can't remember if I was the one who found Arthur Joseph on the day he was dead. I remember that he had white mucous coming from his mouth and nose that day.

Q Did you injure Arthur Joseph in any way?

A: I can't remember if I hurt him or not.

Q: Marie, on each of the times that one of your children was found dead inside of your house, were you alone with the children or was someone else present with you?

A: I was always alone.

Q: Do you remember ever planning on hurting or killing any of your children?

A: No, I don't know why I did it.

Q: Marie, did you realize that there were life insurance policies taken out on the children?

A: Yeah. [It was my] husband, Art. He mostly took out the insurance on them.

Q: Marie, you have stated to us that you were hoping that you would be caught for what you were doing to the children. Why didn't you tell someone back then what you were doing?

A: I don't know. I really don't know. I can't explain why I did what I did.

Q: Did your husband, Arthur Noe, have any knowledge of what was happening to the children either before or after they died?

A: No, I never told Arthur what I did. I don't know what he would do if he found out about what I did, but he would probably never talk to me again.

Q: Marie, is what you have told us in the statement the absolute truth?

A: Yes, as much as I can remember. There are some things that I can't remember.

Q: Do you have any reason why you would harm the children in any way?

A: No, all I can figure is that I'm ungodly sick. I never had the money to get help, and I didn't know where to go for help anyway.

Q: Is there anything else that you would like to add to your statement?

A: No, there's nothing more that I can think of.

After her confession was typed up, Marie read it over and signed it. As the detectives led her out of Interrogation Room D, Marie Noe seemed peaceful, as if a huge weight had been lifted off her broad shoulders after so many years.

"Don't tell my husband what I told youse," she whispered to the detectives, as she was reunited with Arthur at about 5 a.m.

EIGHTEEN

ENDGAME

As Arthur and Marie Noe pondered their future on N. American Street, Marie's confession was sent to D.A. Lynne Abraham's office for review; ultimately it would be her decision whether or not to prosecute. The homicide department was a hive of activity. Secrecy was vital, and detectives were only briefed on a need-to-know basis.

But within a week the news of Marie's confession was leaked to the *Philadelphia Inquirer.* And on April 1, it ran a dramatic front-page story announcing that police had reopened one of Philadelphia's greatest unsolved murder mysteries. Although some readers must have initially wondered if the then-unconfirmed report was some sort of bad-taste April Fool's joke, it soon ignited a national media frenzy.

"The case is under investigation," a spokesperson for Abraham's office told reporters. "And it is a homicide case."

Within hours, hordes of reporters and camera crews descended on N. American Street, camping outside the Noes' shabby row house to question the elderly couple, who invited one local ABC news crew inside for an interview to protest their innocence.

"It haunts you, yes," said a visibly shocked Marie Noe. "If they can find some answers better than what they did when they first passed away, I'd be glad to find out. Not knowing one way or the other."

The following morning millions of viewers learned about Marie Noe and her ten dead children on ABC's *Good Morning America* as the Philadelphia *Daily News* reported that she had signed a confession admitting suffocating four of her babies. The story was followed up by national evening news, *The Washington Post* and *The New York Times*, and the top-rated *Dateline NBC* began preparing a lead story to air the following week.

That day an ambitious Philadelphia defense lawyer named David Rudenstein arrived at the Noes' and offered to take on the high-profile case for nothing. Arthur and Marie, who now were completely out of their depth dealing with the police and media, immediately agreed.

The mustached, overweight lawyer with a penchant for flashy, loose-fitting three-piece-suits, then called a press conference to announce that the Noes had retained his services. Straight off the bat he declared Marie's confession inadmissible, as she had been questioned for eleven hours without an attorney present. Besides, he added, her mental condition on the night she was interrogated nullified the confession.

"[There's] absolutely no evidence of wrongdoing," he declared, adding that he'd never seen anyone confess to four murders and be sent straight home.

Rudenstein was well-known to the district attorney's office as a smart adversary who would go to great lengths to prove a client's point in a courtroom. At one trial he had the jury in stitches, producing a Pinocchio doll to humiliate a witness he had called a liar.

The first thing Rudenstein did was to order the Noes to stop talking to the media. He then lodged an official letter of complaint to the district attorney's office, copies of which he gave to the press.

"The overwhelming pain of having lost these children is something that none of us can possibly understand," it read. "A continuing attack upon this couple through leaks to the media . . . would be nothing short of disgraceful."

For the next five months Marie Noe lay low with her husband in N. American Street, on the instructions of her new attorney. But although the media spotlight was temporarily off the Noes there was much activity in the background to build a cast-iron case against her.

"We were trying to resurrect a fifty-year-old case," said D.A. Lynne Abraham. "Nobody knew about this case. It was off the charts. This was terra incognita."

Her chief of homicide, Charles Gallagher, then began examining the complete set of Joe McGillen's now-faded case files, well aware that many of the damning statements against the Noes could be ruled inadmissible in court if the case made trial.

Many of the vital witnesses were now dead, so it was crucial that the surviving ones agree to testify. Homicide Detectives Steve Vivarina and John McDermott were immediately assigned to track down any witnesses who were still alive and re-interview them. It would prove a long and laborious job, requiring many weeks of telephone calls and public record-checking.

They started on April 14, by interviewing Dr. Abraham Perlman, who, as a young pediatrician forty years earlier, had been told by Marie Noe that the yet-unnamed baby Constance wouldn't survive.

Dr. Perlman, now seventy-four and working as a psychiatric resident in the geriatric department at Norristown State Hospital, had never forgotten his shocking encounter with Marie Noe in February 1958.

"The baby was just a day old and it was a routine exam," said Dr. Perlman. "When I told [Marie] that, she responded, 'She's not going to live. Just like the others.' "

The doctor researched Marie's medical history and ordered a range of tests on Constance, which all turned out normal.

"I told this to the mother," he continued, "and her reaction was that it wouldn't make any difference. [She] seemed indifferent to the whole situation. She shrugged it off with another remark: 'This one wouldn't make it.' After that it stopped being routine."

A month later the two detectives traveled to Virginia, to interview another two surviving key witnesses in the case. It was early afternoon when they arrived at the Middletown home of Theresa Martin, who, as a young policewoman in the Philadelphia Juvenile Aid Division, had interviewed the Noes after Mary Lee's death in January 1963.

Now sixty-six years old and married, the years had not dimmed her memories of Marie Noe. She told the detectives that she definitely had suspicions about Marie murdering her children, which were reinforced by Marie's showing "very little emotion" during questioning.

Vivarina and McDermott then drove fifty miles east along Highway 66 to the town of Vienna. At 5:25 p.m. they drew up in front of the house of Sister Mary Gemma, the pediatric supervisor who became a surrogate mother to Cathy Noe during the months she'd spent in St. Joseph's Hospital. When the homicide investigators told her why they had come, she was still unaware that the case was being re-opened.

Although she had been only twenty-one when she'd cared for little Cathy, thirty-six years ago, the former nun—who has reverted to her former name, Shirley Mendolia—vividly recalled the happy, loving toddler with the curly blonde hair.

"Catherine was so beautiful and a very precious child," she remembered. "I can still see her. I remember the crib she was in." All the St. Joseph's nurses suspected Marie Noe of harming Cathy, the sister said, and were afraid to send her home after each hospitalization. "Everybody watched her like a hawk. We were trying to discover what the mother was doing but we never did."

Four days later the detectives interviewed Violetta Zimba, the neighbor who was summoned by Marie to try and revive baby Constance. Now eighty-four years old and still living in Kensington, Violetta recalled that fateful day, remarking that Marie had been "out in left field."

At midday on June 12, the detectives met William White, the now-retired policeman who had rushed the dying Mary Lee Noe to the hospital. Casting his mind back to that winter's day in 1963, White told Vivarina and McDermott that Marie had been in a "daze" and "like a zombie" during the unsuccessful attempts to save her baby.

After leaving White's house, the detectives drove straight to Pennsylvania, to interview the recently widowed Marie Maxymuik, whose late husband Daniel had once been the Noes' friend and lawyer. It was Mrs. Maxymuik, now seventy, who had taken Cathy Noe to Episcopal Hospital on the day she died. While admitting that there was much neighborhood gossip about what had happened to the Noe babies, Mrs. Maxymuik said she always minded her own business.

"I wasn't really one to socialize," she explained, adding that her son Nicholas used to play with Cathy, as they were the same age.

Four days later Vivarina and McDermott arrived at Children's Hospital to interview Dr. Patrick Pasquariello, who had treated the tenth Noe baby, Little Arty. Now a sixty-seven-year-old senior pediatrician, Dr. Pasquariello had been the head of pediatrics at St. Joseph's Hospital when Dr. Gangemi had placed the new-born baby in his hands in July 1967.

He told the investigators that both he and Dr. Gangemi were suspicious of Marie Noe but none of their tests on Little Arty revealed anything abnormal. Now he was convinced that Marie had suffocated her children.

Two days later Vivarina and McDermott met with retired Detective Vincent Toner, who had been assigned from East Detectives to interview the Noes after Little Arty's death. He told them that Marie had seemed unusually "calm and cool" after he had read her her rights.

"She was no more shook up after I got there, [than] when I left," he said. "[It was] like a normal visit on a normal day."

He added that Detective Joseph Schimpf had never contacted him about his interview during the 1968 investigation which had cleared Marie Noe of any wrongdoing.

Almost a month later the two detectives reconvened to interview the late Dr. Columbus Gangemi's medical assistant, Maria Datillo, at the Philadelphia home of a friend. She recalled Cathy Noe's frequent visits to the office with her mother, and the dreadful day that the little girl died.

It had been Mrs. Datillio, now seventy-one, who had taken the phone call from Marie Noe announcing Cathy's death. She recalled the doctor recoiling with horror at the news, telling her to call the police. But never, to her knowledge, had Dr. Gangemi ever put anything in writing about Marie's possible child abuse.

Three weeks later, at the beginning of August, District Attorney Lynne Abraham conferred with the chief of her homicide unit, Charlie Gallagher, to decide a course of action. All the death certificates and available autopsy reports for the eight Noe babies had been studied by the present Philadelphia medical examiner, Dr. Haresh Mirchandani, and his deputy, Dr. Ian Hood. They had both concluded that the cause of each death was suffocation, and officially ruled them homicide for the first time.

Abraham and Gallagher now decided that they had a strong enough case to proceed and issued a warrant to arrest Marie Noe for serial murder of her children.

In the early morning of Wednesday, August 5, Sergeant Larry Nodiff and Detectives Steve Vivarina and John McDermott arrived at the Noes' house. The tough homicide cops were nervous as they approached the rickety front door with an "N" in the latticework, and knocked.

The elderly couple were still asleep and it took ten minutes of continually ringing the bell and knocking before a sleepy-looking Arthur Noe finally appeared behind the front-door screen, asking what they wanted.

When Sergeant Nodiff informed him they had a warrant for Marie's arrest he looked stunned, asking them to wait while he got Marie up and they got dressed. As the men stood outside the row house, they could hear Arthur trying unsuccessfully to call his lawyer David Rudenstein. Finally he and Marie emerged from the front door, to be led into the back of the detective's black Ford Explorer for the trip downtown.

Neither Marie nor Arthur showed any trace of emotion during the short drive, and Nodiff didn't bother to handcuff his prisoner, as she couldn't have gotten far in her arthritic condition.

There was little traffic so early in the morning on the ten-minute drive to the Roundhouse, but Arthur still criticized the detective's driving, telling him to concentrate. And as they pulled into the basement parking lot at Police Headquarters, Arthur turned sadly toward his wife, saying, "I guess you won't be home for your birthday."

As Marie Noe was led away by the detectives to be booked on eight charges of the first-degree murder of her children, she slowly turned around to give Arthur one last parting look. But there was nothing behind those washed-out blue eyes.

NINETEEN

SPINNING THE CASE

As Marie Noe was being fingerprinted at police headquarters, that morning's *Philadelphia Inquirer* was already on the streets with an exclusive front-page story announcing her imminent arrest. The leak from within the police department would considerably lessen D.A. Lynne Abraham's impact at her press conference, where she described the Noe case as "a wake-up call to doctors and law enforcement agencies."

The well-informed story, bearing the banner headline "Charges to be Filed in Infants' Death," quoted an unnamed investigator saying that Marie Noe had "taken responsibility" for murdering some of her babies and could be arrested as early as today.

"I'm sure [the Noes] are not happy to see all this tragedy bubble up again," Dr. Halbert Fillinger told the *Inquirer*. "But I think it is a good idea. I still think something must have happened to those kids."

Marie Noe's arrest dominated that evening's local and national television news and by the next morning it was reported in *The Washington Post*, *The New York Times* and the *Los Angeles Times*, as well as scores of other papers as far afield as Europe and Asia.

For the first time in thirty-five years Marie Noe was firmly back in the national spotlight, but this time it was not as a bereaved martyr but as an evil monster.

The head of the Philadelphia Police Homicide Division, Inspector Jerrold Kane, told reporters that the Noe case was possibly the largest number of deaths attributed to crib death in a single family in America.

"This is certainly a unique and bizarre investigation," declared Kane. "The children have always deserved their day in court, and now they will get it."

The Noes' attorney David Rudenstein immediately jumped into the fray, voicing concern over Marie's health and hoping that she did not "drop dead."

"They have lost ten children," he told reporters, adding that his client would be pleading innocent. "They are broke. I've chosen to represent her, but there are no assets to pay counsel. I'm doing it *pro bono*."

Then he went on the attack, claiming that police had denied Marie Noe counsel during the March interrogation and refused to provide a doctor when she had requested one for a headache.

"Even if we take everything the D.A.'s Office says as true," said Rudenstein, "it's clear Mrs. Noe would be a very, very sick woman. If they were interested in seeking help for her, that could have been done in another fashion. If the district attorney's only interest is a big splash case, if the only goal is to incarcerate her for the rest of her life, I am personally appalled and disgusted."

Turning his attention to Arthur Noe, who had not been charged with anything, Rudenstein said: "I haven't seen anyone look worse and still be breathing."

As Marie Noe spent her first night behind bars in solitary confinement, her tearful husband returned home alone to discover that police had ransacked their house, seizing all the baby pictures, birth certificates and anything else involving the children. The living room walls were punctuated by large square dust marks where Cathy Noe's pictures had hung for more than a generation.

"They took everything," said Marie's eighty-year-old sister Anne Danielski, who remained convinced of her innocence. "They're trying to make her into a monster. It makes me *so* mad."

The morning after her arrest, Marie Noe was taken to the justice center for preliminary arraignment. The ultra-modern, fourteen-story complex of courts, across from City Hall, had been open just two years. This would be its most high-profile case to date.

During her brief court appearance, bail was denied and she was returned to her solitary cell, as Rudenstein lodged an emergency appeal to the municipal court.

"For the past thirty years, Mrs. Noe has led an extremely quiet life in the West Kensington section of the city," Rudenstein wrote in his sixteen-point appeal for bail. "She has harmed no one. No reasonable person could say that she is a prospective harm to anyone."

News of Marie Noe's arrest was received with stunned disbelief on the streets of Kensington. The tightly-knit row house neighborhood immediately sprang to her defense, searching for reasons why one of their own should be accused of such a heinous crime.

"I couldn't believe it," said thirty-four-year-old Robin Gredone, who told the *Philadelphia Inquirer* that she used to stop at the Noes' home for candy as a child. "Why, after all these years, all of a sudden, it's coming up again. That's ridiculous. If they were going to do anything about it, they should have done it back then. What's she going to do? Die in prison?"

Another neighbor, Kathryn Reinhardt, who had taken

up a collection in the neighborhood after one of the babies' deaths, said that everyone believed the children had died of crib death.

"Back in those days you didn't mistrust people like you do today," said the eighty-five-year-old, who had lived at the corner of Tioga and N. American Streets for more than half a century. "Today I wouldn't trust my next-door neighbors."

Police told Arthur Noe he would not be able to visit his wife in jail for a whole week, although he could receive a daily collect telephone call from her. Heartbroken, he would spend the long hours alone in his front room, occasionally venturing out onto the front stoop for a cigarette, but never straying too far in case he missed Marie's daily phone call. And as the full weight of what was happening to him and Marie sunk in, Arthur's thoughts turned to suicide.

On the Friday after the arrest Associated Press reporter Meki Cox and a photographer arrived at N. American Street on a sweltering hot afternoon to find Arthur distraught and suicidal. The front door was open and the lonely, emaciated old man peered through the screen with tears in his eyes.

"We came up and asked him if he was OK," said Cox. "Then he just went back inside the house."

They followed him inside to the front room, which was dirty and smelled of cat urine. Now at his lowest ebb, Arthur sat down in his vinyl recliner next to Marie's empty chair, and burst into tears as he started unburdening himself. His voice cracking with emotion, he announced his intention to buy a gun and blow his head off, saying that it was the only way he'd ever see his kids again.

"I never saw them ride a bike," he sobbed. "I never saw them with a boyfriend."

Concerned for his safety, Cox sent the photographer out to a nearby bodega to get him a cold beer, while she tried to talk him out of committing suicide.

"I sat there and started talking to him," she said. "He stopped talking about a gun and I asked him about his family and children. It was amazing. He just started right from the beginning and the first child and then spoke about each one and how they died."

By the time he had finished the story of Little Arty's death, he had stopped crying and composed himself. Then, as if in pain, he picked up a suicide note from the floor that he had been writing before they arrived, and let them read it.

"Dearest Marie," the note read. "I can't go on anymore. You are my life, my love. Without you there is no life."

Cox and the photographer stayed with him for two hours, worried that he might kill himself. At one point large tears started rolling down his craggy cheeks as he wrapped himself in a dirty bed sheet, sobbing, "This is one hell of a way to live."

Continually, he protested his wife's innocence, saying he would have turned her in if he'd believed she'd killed their children.

"I've lived with this woman fifty years," he said, jabbing the air with a cigarette to make his point. "That woman was not capable of doing such a thing. She wouldn't harm a fly. She was my life."

Then he picked up the suicide note and continued writing: "All I wanted to do was grow old with you and our memories, but for fate I now know that is not to be. I will never stop loving you. Love, Art."

On the way back to the Associated Press office, Cox was so concerned that she stopped off at the local police station, asking the duty officer to keep an eye on Arthur, as he was suicidal. She also called a suicide hotline, who agreed to help. Then she put in a telephone call to David Rudenstein to warn him that she would be writing a story about what had happened.

The following day Cox returned to N. American Street and found Arthur fully recovered and back to his old argumentative self. His morale had been bolstered by a pep talk from Rudenstein, who had told him that he must be strong for his wife.

While Marie Noe languished in her cell, there was a bitter battle going on in the media over which publication had put her there. *Philadelphia* magazine and its senior reporter, now editor, Stephen Fried claimed credit for breaking the thirty-year-old case, but the *Daily News*, who had carried the original story in January, said *it* was responsible.

"The credit belongs to the outfit that got the story into print first," *Daily News* editor Zack Stalberg told Philadelphia's *City Paper*. "Nobody is trying to deny the magazine credit. We didn't know they deserve the credit."

Fried, who had appeared on *Dateline NBC* and other national cable programs to discuss the case, soon fired back, saying: "Getting the story into print first did not re-activate the [Noe] case."

A few days later Marie's sister Anne arrived in Philadelphia to visit and found Arthur Noe lying unconscious on the floor, being revived by neighbors. He was soon brought around and Anne decided to stay for a few days and take care of him.

The following Wednesday she accompanied Arthur to Room 306 at the Criminal Justice Center for the preliminary hearing. Marie remained in prison as her two closest relations sat in the second row to hear Rudenstein request bail and additional time to prepare his case.

Rudenstein told Municipal Court Judge Eric L. Lilian that Arthur Noe was deeply depressed and suicidal. He might die unless Marie was freed on bail.

"I am concerned about Arthur," said the huge, boyish-looking lawyer, as he arrived in his tan Pontiac with the emaciated Arthur, to be greeted by scores of reporters and photographers. "He's vital to her defense. If he drops dead, it will be extremely detrimental."

Later that morning Judge Lilian refused bail but agreed to postpone the preliminary hearing for a further two weeks until August 26, to allow Rudenstein additional time to prepare his defense. After the brief hearing Arthur Noe looked shaken and unsteady as Rudenstein guided him past the line of reporters, firing a barrage of questions about his wife and children.

The following day Arthur arrived at the jail to visit Marie for the first time since her arrest. As he was running late and had to fill out the necessary paperwork first, he had only half an hour alone with his wife.

"We thought it was important for Marie to see her husband alone," explained Anne Danielski. "He's taking it very badly."

Four days later Rudenstein took Arthur Noe to the studios of WWDB–FM to appear on Irv Homer's top-rated Philadelphia talk show. Sounding on the verge of tears, his voice shaking with emotion, Noe staunchly defended his wife to Homer's radio audience.

"I'll fight to the death to show she never harmed them," he said. "She's my friend, my companion. The most beautiful woman in the world for me."

Then he bemoaned the fact that he would never see his children ride a bike or go to school or tell him, "Daddy, I love you," adding that he often thought about how many grandchildren and even great-grandchildren he might have had if his babies had lived.

The following Sunday, August 23, Marie Noe celebrated her seventieth birthday alone behind bars, wondering if she would ever see the light of day again.

"We sent her cards," said her sister Anne. "But that's where she spent her birthday. It was terrible. What in the world are they trying to do to that woman?"

Three days later, Judge Carolyn Engel Temin freed Marie on $500,000 bail, deciding that she was no longer a threat to anyone. The judge also felt there was no danger of Marie fleeing, as the couple were on the poverty-line, with a fixed income of only $1,600 a month. The D.A.'s chief of homicide, Charles Gallagher, had opposed bail because of the seriousness of the crime and the likelihood that she would be convicted. "We do have eight innocent souls that were killed," he pointed out.

But Judge Temin overruled him, saying that Marie had always fully cooperated with the police. As a condition of her bail, she was ordered to wear an electronic monitoring ankle bracelet, and stay inside her home except to visit her doctor and attorney.

During the hearing Arthur had sat wedged between his wife and sister-in-law, clasping his hands in prayer.

On hearing the judge's ruling, he burst into tears and became so emotional that he had to be comforted by Anne Danielski. Later, as he left the courtroom, he blew a kiss to Marie and kissed a spectator's hand.

"My prayers have been answered," he told the reporters waiting outside the courthouse. "I've been doing terrible through all this. Now, I'm elated."

Then Rudenstein drove the jubilant couple home where they found another battalion of reporters and camera crews on their doorstep. Holding a cigarette in an arthritic hand, Arthur told them he was on "cloud nine," declaring it the "happiest day of [his] life."

"It's been an emotionally draining day," said Rudenstein, ushering Arthur and Marie through their front door. "She thanked her husband. She thanked me. She thanked God. The best thing for her to do now is to rest and clear her mind."

After the couple had disappeared inside the house to be alone together for the first time since the arrest three weeks earlier, Anne Danielski appealed to reporters to give them some peace.

"When you get old, you're just glad to have somebody with you," she said. "The whole family is gone now, so who else do they have?"

A few days after Marie's release, Arthur Noe placed a telephone call to the State Correctional Institution in Huntingdon to ask an old friend for a favor. Richard Riebow, who was presently serving five to ten years for robbery, had known the Noes for years and was a regular at Arthur's favorite taproom. On hearing of Marie's arrest, he was only too happy to help his old friend and, three months before he himself was released on parole, wrote a letter to the editor of the Philadelphia *Daily News*, which duly appeared in its opinion page.

Titled, "Mrs. Noe a Killer? It's Unbelievable," Riebow's letter began, "People should come forth and express their concerns about the witch hunt in the Marie Noe case." Stating that he had grown up a block from the Noes and known them for over twenty-two years, Riebow wrote the "hopelessness, loss and pain" they suffered after the death of their children was unimaginable.

He then attacked Lynn Abraham's office for going on a "witch hunt," citing examples of the generosity the Noes displayed toward him as a child and how they were "all-around good neighbors."

Riebow then questioned why the investigators in the 1960s had never found anything wrong, claiming Marie Noe was merely a scapegoat for new findings on Sudden Infant Death Syndrome.

"I do not believe Mrs. Noe could, would or did kill her children."

When the district attorney's office read the letter, it was livid. Charles Gallagher immediately filed a motion in court and was granted a gag order, preventing anyone involved in the Marie Noe case from talking to the media until further notice.

TWENTY

LIE LIKE A LOG

Back at home Marie Noe was at the end of her tether and, like her husband, her thoughts turned to suicide. She contemplated stabbing herself to death with a butcher's knife or taking an overdose of pills. But she could never go through with it.

"Poor Marie, she's just ready to pull out that little bit of hair she has left," said her sister Anne, who made frequent visits to Philadelphia from her home in Reading, Pennsylvania, to look after the couple. "It's very bad for her." Of course Arthur was delighted to have his wife home again but there was an uneasy truce between the elderly couple, with Marie still staunchly maintaining her innocence and Arthur not being able to face up to the reality of being married to a serial killer.

"It's a type of denial," explains Dallas forensic pathologist Dr. Linda Norton, who is an infanticide expert. "The spouse wants so much to believe in this person, that they have come to depend upon, that they're willing to leave their common sense behind and simply believe. And it doesn't make any difference how obvious it may be to other individuals around. It's like, 'I'm not going to believe it because I don't want to.' "

And after so many years in denial about Marie, justifying his children's deaths as acts of God, Arthur must now have secretly suspected his wife: when Marie had been arrested he timidly asked a detective if he thought she had really killed his children.

But fifty years of marriage had left him *so* dependent on Marie and *so* scared of losing her, that he could never challenge her. It would mean tearing them apart and having to spend his final days alone. There was a dreadful co-dependency between the couple with their very survival at stake. From now on they would both do whatever was necessary to block out the truth and stay together.

Over the next weeks and months their crumbling house on N. American Street became their prison as they played a macabre game of charades. Pretending that Marie was innocent was a game that had to be kept up at all costs. There was the added pressure of their lawyer David Rudenstein, who was already telling the press that he couldn't continue working for nothing forever.

On October 7, 1998, the Noes drove to the Criminal Justice Center, where Marie signed a form to officially waive her preliminary hearing. The scheduled two-day hearing, which the district attorney's office had put Dr. Molly Dapena, Joe McGillen and Dr. Halbert Fillinger on stand-by to attend, was then abruptly canceled.

A week later another brief hearing was held where Judge Carolyn Temin ordered Marie Noe to undergo a complete psychiatric evaluation to decide if she was mentally competent to stand trial on eight counts of murder.

At 2:30 p.m. on Friday, November 6, Marie Noe returned to the Criminal Justice Center to be examined by two court-appointed psychiatrists, Dr. John O'Brien and Dr. Robert L. Sadoff. Eager to make a good impression, she had put on her best dress and applied some light make-up and lipstick to her pallid features. She appeared alert and cooperative as she shuffled into a conference room with a cane to find Dr. Sadoff already waiting for her. He then engaged her in casual conversation until Dr. O'Brien arrived fifteen minutes later. Although the two psychiatrists were at a disadvantage, not having received copies of her confession and Joe McGillen's detailed 1963 and 1968 investigations, they pressed ahead anyway.

They warned Marie that they would be taking notes and that the traditional doctor–patient confidentiality wouldn't apply in this case.

For the next two-and-a-half-hours, Marie discussed the deaths of her ten children, speaking candidly about her marriage and her own questionable state of mind. She enjoyed being the center of attention as the two doctors probed her tortuous mind.

Throughout the session Marie was well aware that the doctors would be deciding her mental competency to stand trial and that it could mean the difference between being sent to a hospital or spending the rest of her life in jail.

The doctors began by asking Marie about her confession and she immediately claimed that the police had coerced her into making it. She explained that during her eleven-hour interrogation, she had developed a migraine but was forbidden to take her medicine. "[They] were very good at their jobs," she said dispassionately, claiming she had only signed the statement after being told that she could then go home with Arthur.

Tears welled up in her eyes as she told the doctors

how she would now resort to any means to save her marriage.

"I would lie like a log if I have to," she boldly declared. "If I had to I would say I did something to those kids to stay out of jail. They had me in such a complexing [sic] situation. I'd say anything to get the devil out of that room."

But when the doctors later read her confession they agreed that it had been made voluntarily, without any "prompting or prodding" by the detectives, who had not been in any way aggressive with their questioning.

When asked about her children, Marie became evasive, saying she did not remember specific details about their deaths. At first she could only discuss one of them clearly and was vague on the others.

Questioned about her several alleged rapes in 1949 and 1954, she gave versions totally different from the accounts she had previously made in sworn statements to police. Although she'd claimed in 1949 that she'd been raped by a black man, she no longer could remember his race. And in the second attack she now claimed that there had been no sexual contact with the intruder, who had bound her up with Arthur's ties and left her lying helplessly under the bed.

"She is apparently a fairly poor historian," wrote Dr. Sadoff in his subsequent report. "There is therefore, an inconsistency in her memory pattern."

Marie was then asked about her miserable childhood in Kensington and her relationship with her parents. There was a rush of emotion as she told the psychiatrists that she had been a sickly child and, being the youngest, was always the family scapegoat. She said her parents had physically punished her on frequent occasions, beating her with "a cat-o'-nine tails, with a closed fist and with a belt" on her buttocks.

"You didn't have the kind of life I had," she said sadly, as if looking for sympathy.

Asked about sexual abuse as a child, she replied, "No, no, no, not really unless I volunteered it."

She described her early sexual experiences as a fourteen-year-old, when she had run off to Florida with an older neighbor to attend her niece's funeral. She admitted trading sexual favors for the car ride south. Then she owned up to having had at least one affair in the early days of her marriage, after meeting a man in a taproom. She said she had felt so guilty afterwards, that she had told Arthur, who forgave her, after making her see a doctor to check for venereal disease.

The doctors then asked about her present life, since returning home from jail. Marie said that she was eating well and had no problem sleeping. She did not have "nightmares or bad dreams." She also denied ever hearing voices or seeing visions.

The doctors then brought up her temporary blindness after the death of each child. Although the 1949 psychiatric reports showed that her first attack of blindness occurred after the death of her first child, Richard Allen, when she had been diagnosed with "conversion hysteria," Marie now claimed that they had actually begun after she had lost her third baby, Jacqueline. It had resulted, she said, in her being hospitalized overnight for observation.

Wrote Dr. Sadoff: "She described herself as being completely blind, but did not see black and white, only 'blank.' It was later clarified that she could distinguish light and dark, but no forms or figures."

Marie told them that on each subsequent occasion she went blind for short periods but always knew it would soon pass. She also now claimed to have suffered frequent blackouts with her migraine headaches, although denying ever having head injuries or suffering seizures or epilepsy.

When Dr. Sadoff brought up the current state of her marriage, Marie became emotional. She told them she and Arthur had recently celebrated their golden wedding anniversary and that although their present relationship was "topsy-turvy," it would survive.

Questioned about her sex life with Arthur, Marie said that the couple had had a very active one which always stopped about six weeks after the birth of each baby.

"She described the baby as giving excitement to their lives," wrote Dr. Sadoff in his report. "And that when the baby died she felt 'empty.' "

She told doctors that she and Arthur had stopped having sexual relations in March, after doctors warned he might have prostate cancer.

Asked to describe a typical day in her life, Marie said she got up at 6:30 a.m. and did the self-hypnosis exercises she had learned from Dr. Gangemi, before making breakfast for Arthur and reading the morning paper. The rest of the day was spent reading, watching television and drinking beer. Telling the doctors that she was forbidden to leave home, she looked anxiously at the clock, saying she had to leave soon.

In the early days of their marriage, said Marie, she and Arthur would go to the local taproom with friends and drink a lot of beer and get drunk. They would never drive, but walk home. She said somebody had told her that the occasional glass of wine would be good for her low blood pressure but she never touched hard liquor or street drugs. On a typical day, she said, they might have three cans of beer apiece in front of the television.

Suddenly, Marie brought up an upcoming court hearing, saying she had no idea what it was for, as she still had not officially pleaded guilty or not guilty. She then told the doctors that she presumed they were examining her to decide if she was "unstable" or "suicidal." If she was certified unstable she would go to a hospital but if found competent she might be sent to jail.

"As a result of her response," Dr. Sadoff later reported, "I asked her about suicidal ideation. And she said she often thinks about it, but she has never tried and doesn't believe she ever will try."

When asked what method she would use, Marie immediately replied, "with a butcher knife to the stomach." She added that she had a lot of prescribed medicines at home that she could take, but didn't want to go that route.

Describing Arthur as "a very fragile man," Marie said he couldn't survive without her and that was why she couldn't take her own life. She expressed her deep concern about how dependent he was on her, adding that he would be devastated if she had to spend the rest of her life in jail.

"We need each other," she sobbed. "We are dependent on each other. I'd do anything to help my husband."

Then she said she'd prefer jail to being home alone without Arthur, as she had no friends. At least in jail, she thought, there would be other prisoners to relate to.

The doctors then segued to why she had continued having so many children. Marie said that she had wanted to have her tubes tied at one point, but her parish priest had told her that it would be a sin and to follow God's will and procreate. Recently, she added, she and Arthur had stopped going to church altogether as her husband felt St. Hugh's was "going the Spanish way."

Returning to her confession, Marie now admitted that she could have been telling the truth about smothering her babies with a pillow. She claimed not to remember anything about the deaths of some of her babies, but could recall others.

"I supposedly suffocated him," she said, referring to her first child, Richard Allen. "[The police] were very persuasive men."

She was able to tell the doctors that Mary Lee died a crib death; Terry died forty-eight hours after birth in the hospital; Cathy succumbed on the way to the hospital, after being in the playpen; and Little Arty had died on the sofa.

"When asked specifically about the deaths of her children," wrote Dr. Sadoff, "Mrs. Noe states that she does not remember killing them, but admits that it is possible that she could have smothered them and not remembered because it would be so horrible for her. When I asked why she could make statements about four of the children and not all of them, she said that some she just doesn't remember at all, and the others she remembers and was open to the possibility that she could have killed them, although she does not specifically remember smothering them."

When the doctors asked if she had liked being a mother, Marie admitted finding the demands of caring for an infant "challenging." She said various family members would help her out when it became too stressful. But she told the doctors that she had "enjoyed" her children and liked bathing and feeding them and even changing their "smelly diapers." She described motherhood as "a joy and a challenge."

Then the doctors asked her about why she had wanted to adopt a child, after losing so many of her own. She said she and Arthur had first started thinking about adoption before her hysterectomy in 1967. She had believed she would have better luck in raising a child if it was not their own.

She described her life without her children as "dull" and surprised the doctors by saying that she would like to have been a nurse or a doctor if she had only been better educated.

As part of her mental evaluation Marie Noe was given a formal cognitive capacity screening examination by Dr. O'Brien, where she was shown four items and asked to remember them. Five minutes later, when she was unable to recall them, the doctors prompted her with erroneous answers which she immediately accepted. This revealed how easily suggestible she could be, and how susceptible she was to other people's ideas.

She became anxious when asked to do simple mental calculations, like giving numbers backwards and forwards. She found it difficult to reverse a sequence of numbers, although she was able to give them forwards. She explained that she had always been very poor at math, although she did manage to perform simple sums successfully.

Her basic spelling skills seemed to be good and she was able to spell the word "world" both backwards and forwards. And her general knowledge was also good as she correctly named the President and Vice-President of the United States, as well as the name of the Governor of Pennsylvania.

"She exhibited intact abstract and conceptual thinking," noted Dr. O'Brien. "[An] intact ability to follow verbal and written commands and intact superficial social judgments."

But when she was given the Minnesota Multiphasic Personality Inventory test (MMPI) by Dr. O'Brien, Marie Noe's true personality finally emerged for the first time. The MMPI is the standard test to measure personality and is used regularly by five thousand American companies to screen hiring possibilities.

It consists of five hundred carefully worded questions to be answered "yes" or "no." A sample MMPI test included a range of questions like:

I believe my sins are unpardonable.
When you are in low spirits do you try and find someone to cheer you up?
Do ideas run through your head so you cannot sleep?
Do you feel that marriage is essential to your present or future happiness?

The test deliberately plants several "lie" questions which are repeated several times. If an attempt is made to "cheat" the test, by giving the answers that the subject feels the test designers are looking for, that "desire to please" is clearly revealed in the results.

When Dr. O'Brien evaluated Marie Noe's MMPI test results he found that she exhibited "significant histrionic personality traits." He found she would use anything at her disposal, such as her children or her bouts of blindness, to deliberately "manipulate" her family and doctors into getting her own way.

Dr. O'Brien also found Marie narcissistic and very self-conscious about her physical appearance and how she was perceived by others. She also displayed "psychopathic deviate tendencies," reflecting the conflicts and discomfort she felt in her interpersonal relationships as well as a "resentment of societal standards."

At the end of the afternoon session, the doctors asked Marie what her three wishes would be, if she could have anything she wanted. Marie said that she would love to get three children back but then corrected herself, saying she would like all five. On being reminded that she had lost ten children and not five, she replied, "Well, two [I] can't get back because one was stillborn, one was dead after forty-eight hours."

But she remained with five children, as if her others had never existed. Asked which five babies she wanted back, Marie began to name them but then became confused and gave up.

Dr. Sadoff then made a further appointment to see Marie Noe on November 17, so that in the meantime, he could obtain a full set of reports from the district attorney's office to compare to Marie's answers.

David Rudenstein accompanied Marie Noe to her second evaluation at the Criminal Justice Center. This time Dr. O'Brien was not present. Dr. Sadoff sat across the conference table from Rudenstein and his client. It now appeared that her attorney had changed strategy with a view to making a plea.

"I had so many blackouts [that] I might have killed all eight," she immediately declared, adding that she still couldn't recall the specifics of exactly how they died.

Asked about her first two children, Richard and Elizabeth, Marie said she remembered telling the police that she had smothered both of them, Richard in his bassinet and Elizabeth with a pillow. She said she could not remember how her third baby, Jacqueline, had died but her fourth child, Arthur Jr., had turned blue. When Dr. Sadoff asked about Constance, Marie coolly replied: "I could possibly be responsible for her death as well."

Then, in the presence of her lawyer, Marie said that despite her previous reservations about the length of her interrogation, her confession "could still have been the truth."

"[I] had no awareness that I had done anything wrong to them," she said. "[I] must have pushed it out of my mind." She claimed that long-repressed memories of smothering her children had only surfaced during the interrogation.

"I feel disgusted with myself," Marie said when asked how she felt after finally admitting to having murdered her children. She claimed there must be something wrong with her psychologically, though she had never before believed that she suffered from mental problems. But as she had accepted that *she* had been the one causing her children's deaths, so she accepted that she must be mentally ill.

She then told Dr. Sadoff that she wanted psychiatric care to help her explore what had led her to murder her babies—not only for herself but so she could help other desperate mothers in similar positions.

"[I] want to redeem [myself] by helping others in this matter," she declared magnanimously.

Blaming the killings on the frequent blackouts during

her migraine attacks, she said that she had not experienced any further ones since her hysterectomy in 1968. Her temporary memory losses, she reasoned, must explain why she had forgotten that she killed her children, and she still could not remember exact details of their deaths. Saying she now felt "guilt and remorse" for her actions, she told Dr. Sadoff that she was now facing up to reality.

The following day the two psychiatrists sent their mental evaluation of Marie Noe to Charles Gallagher at the district attorney's office. They included full accounts of their interviews and findings on whether she was competent to stand trial, but the doctors disagreed on what treatment she should receive.

Dr. O'Brien diagnosed Marie Noe as suffering from "Mixed Personality Disorder with dependent, histrionic and narcissistic features." But he ruled out dissociative amnesia caused by her alleged blackouts.

He wrote: "At the present time, Mrs. Noe is able to understand the nature and object of the proceedings against her and to participate and assist in her own defense. It is therefore my opinion that she is currently competent to stand trial."

The doctor added that he was "troubled" by Marie's retraction of her confession but this was completely consistent with her personality profile, as provided by the MMPI test. He also found that the police interrogation "did not appear to be unduly stressful or grueling" but that she was "significantly suggestible."

In Dr. O'Brien's opinion, Marie Noe was unlikely to benefit from any psychiatric treatment or medications this late in her life, and was not a danger to anyone as she no longer had access to small children.

Dr. Sadoff admitted that he found it difficult to make a diagnosis, although Marie no longer appeared to be psychotic. He noted her present tearful depression as a result of realizing that she had murdered her eight babies.

"In order to treat the depression," he wrote, "and to deal with the awareness of her responsibility for the deaths of her children, I would strongly recommend regular, intensive treatment for Mrs. Noe. She may require medication as well to help her depression, but certainly she should have the availability for proper psychotherapy. Prognosis for improvement is guarded at this time."

EPILOGUE

On Monday, June 28th, 1999, Marie Noe pleaded guilty to eight counts of the second-degree murders of her children under the 1939 Pennsylvania Penal Code. Her dramatic plea bargain came after months of delicate negotiations between her lawyer David Rudenstein and the Philadelphia District Attorney's Office.

Holding a large folder of her court papers, wearing a pastel blue woolen twin-set in a sweltering heat wave, the self-confessed baby-killer slowly hobbled into the Criminal Justice Center using a cane. Around her ankle was the electronic monitoring bracelet.

Standing between her husband and sister Anne, Marie Noe finally admitted publicly that she had systematically murdered her eight children in cold blood.

"She was shaking like a leaf," said her sister Anne. "We all thought she was going to collapse."

Sitting next to his wife was Arthur Noe, who looked a beaten man, his head slumped into his hands. He grimaced as if in pain as Marie admitted that she was guilty of "repeated acts of infanticide, i.e. killing my children."

There was little emotion in her voice as she answered each of Common Pleas Court Judge William J. Mazzola's questions with a deliberate "yes" or "no," and then waited to be officially sentenced for her crimes.

Under the prearranged deal, Judge Mazzola placed her on twenty years' probation on condition that she serve the first five years under house arrest, wearing her monitoring bracelet. She was also ordered to undergo intense monthly psychiatric evaluation to try and determine her motives for committing such a despicable crime.

Ironically, by escaping prison, Marie Noe will once again undoubtedly enjoy being the center of attention as a psychiatric guinea pig, this time to unlock the mystery of serial infanticide.

But infanticide expert Dr. Stuart Asch, who has studied the Marie Noe case and had been asked to provide expert opinion had it gone to trial, dismissed the idea that Marie's inhuman experiences could ever be of benefit to the medical community.

"It doesn't make sense," he said. "Marie Noe killed her babies in order to get other people involved with her. You can't instruct other mothers not to be sick like that."

Dr. Asch believes that serial baby-killers like Marie Noe are in a class of their own. He differentiates them from mothers who kill one baby in a post-partum depression and even ones suffering from Munchausen's Syndrome-By-Proxy.

"They are schizoids who are emotionally severed from society, narcissistic, self-involved and untreatable," he explains. "They can't be approached in psychotherapy because they can't relate to a therapist. There isn't any medication for what they have."

After the sentencing Philadelphia District Attorney Lynne Abraham said that, although it "was a less than perfect" result, it was the best judgment possible. "There needed to be some resolution," Abraham said, explaining the difficulties she faced resurrecting the fifty-year-old case. "We know finally and for all time that her children were killed by her intentionally. And she admitted under oath to the whole world that she was in fact the one who did it without justification, without mitigation and without excuse."

Although there was outrage that Lynne Abraham had settled for such an apparently lenient sentence for the most prolific baby-killer in American history, her deputy district attorney Charles Gallagher said it was "humane" and finally brought closure after so many years.

"We didn't have the strongest case," he said. "You're not going to get these babies back but maybe we'll learn why she did it. Maybe after a long series of treatments, we'll get to the bottom of it. Which is important. Very important."

Outside the court a crestfallen Arthur Noe waved an unlit cigarette at reporters, saying he had no comment.

"Don't think I'm mean," he said on the verge of tears, "but I've had enough."

The irrepressible David Rudenstein, who had advised Marie to admit the killings to find peace and therefore avoid a drawn-out trial which she could not pay for, tried to put the best possible spin on the guilty plea.

"I don't know any other person accused of this type of crime in the history of the world who has ever come forward to work with doctors the way this woman is willing to," he said. "This is not one of those situations where you have the heart of a killer."

As Marie and Arthur Noe drove back to N. American Street, some wondered if she had managed to cheat the system yet again by escaping prison. But Lynne Abraham had found herself between a rock and a hard place, because there was no guarantee that any jury would have convicted such a frail-looking senior citizen and sent her to jail for the rest of her life.

"Had we gone to trial," said Abraham, "and had we not been successful because of the passage of time and the absence of witnesses and evidence, people would be criticizing us for pursuing and persecuting this poor aged lady. So one must do what one must and this was the right outcome in this case."

Before the hearing, the district attorney's office had consulted Dr. Halbert Fillinger, who had been involved in the case for forty years. He believes that sending Marie Noe to prison for the rest of her life would do little good and be a waste of the taxpayers' money.

"There's an awful lot of tough cookies in a women's prison and she just would not live more than a few days," he said the day after sentencing. "She's been her own prison for fifty years so I don't think we lost much. Sometimes these things are better left up to God to adjudicate."

Also in court was Joe McGillen, the tenacious investigator for the medical examiner's office, whose dogged pursuit of Marie Noe all those years ago had culminated in her being brought to justice. Although calling her crimes "bizarre and terrible," McGillen said he was satisfied with the final outcome.

"I don't have any feelings of joy or elation," he said. "After all these years in this long haul these children have finally had their day in court."

But even as Arthur and Marie shut their front door on the world to live out their own private hell, they still remained in heavy denial. For even though he knows his wife murdered his children, Arthur Noe still cannot confront the terrible reality and risk losing her.

"Art's still behind her," said Anne Danielski, who still believes in her sister's innocence. "When this all started he made a public statement that he would have turned her in if he thought Marie had done it. He has not changed at all."

Against all logic, Anne still blames her younger sister's misfortune on a conspiracy of "so-called doctors and their nurses," who deliberately lied to destroy Marie.

"She's innocent," she explained after the sentencing. "Marie is a very mild person, a very caring person who never raised her voice or got into any trouble. As they had no money to pay for a long trial, her lawyer told her that it was the only way she could have peace."

On a sunny afternoon a few months earlier, I braved the mean streets of Kensington to visit the Noes. When I arrived I found Arthur and Marie huddled in their crumbling front room watching television, as if under siege. After repeated knocks at the front door, Arthur Noe finally pulled back the screen to see who it was. A cigarette butt dangled from his nicotine-stained fingers.

"Do you know how long they've kept us in here?" he yelled angrily. "They're doing us a great injustice."

He refused to talk about their present life of limbo, referring all questions to their attorney, David Rudenstein.

"He's our guardian," added the pathetic-looking old man, as he closed the screen and returned to Marie, who was sitting on her armchair by the front window, her ankle monitoring bracelet clearly visible on her ankle.

During the taxi ride back through the bleak badlands of Kensington, I thought back to all the children who had died. The first two would be older than I am now.

One can only guess how their lives might have turned out if their mother had allowed them to live. Perhaps they would have been able to break out of Kensington and go out into the world to make successes of themselves. Maybe they would have married and had their own children and even grandchildren by now. One can only speculate.

D.A. Lynne Abraham was certainly right when she described the Noes as a great American tragedy.

Now, as long as they live, Marie and Arthur Noe will be locked together in a desperate co-dependency with its own warped rules of survival. Marie can never dare admit that she killed the children to Arthur, who in turn can never accuse her.

In their bizarre world the truth is the biggest enemy and can *never* be faced at any cost.

BIBLIOGRAPHY

Chenery, Susan, *Talking Dirty*. Sceptre, 1997.

Eggington, Joyce, *From Cradle to the Grave*. William Morrow, 1989.

Firstman, Richard and Talan, Jamie, *The Death of Innocents*. Bantam Books, October 1997.

Fried, Steven, "From the Cradle to the Grave," *Philadelphia Magazine*, April 1998.

THEY WENT FROM PRAYING TO PREYING...

For I Have Sinned

True Stories of Clergy Who Kill

John Glatt

Priests, pastors, ministers, and nuns: they are the men and women of God. We trust them unconditionally, tell them our darkest deeds, turn to them in our most desperate hour. We would never, in our wildest dreams, expect them to be...cold-blooded murderers. Now, peek into the confessionals of eleven clergy men and women who did the unthinkable—who broke the most sacred commandment: Thou shalt not kill.